Bride's
BOXES

Bride's BOXES

How to Make Decorative Containers for Special Occasions

Pat Oxenford

Photography by Randy Westley

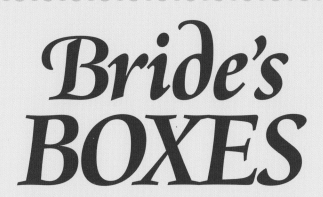

STACKPOLE BOOKS

To my parents, the late Paul R. Krause and Alethea I. Kennedy Krause,
in honor of my Pennsylvania German heritage,
and also to my husband Ray and children Kelly and Michael.

Copyright ©2011 by Stackpole Books

Published by
STACKPOLE BOOKS
5067 Ritter Road
Mechanicsburg, PA 17055
www.stackpolebooks.com

Printed in the United States of America

10 9 8 7 6 5 4 3 2 1

FIRST EDITION

Cover design by Wendy Reynolds

Library of Congress Cataloging-in-Publication Data

Oxenford, Pat.
    Bride's boxes : how to make decorative containers for special occasions /
Pat Oxenford ; photography by Randy Westley. — 1st ed.
        p.   cm.
    Includes bibliographical references (p.   ).
    ISBN-13: 978-0-8117-0563-9 (pbk.)
    ISBN-10: 0-8117-0563-3 (pbk.)
    1. Bride's boxes—Patterns.   I. Title.
TT385.O93   2011
684'.08—dc22

                                                    2011010540

Contents

Acknowledgments

Many people have been instrumental in the publication of this book. First I must thank editor Kyle Weaver, whose confidence in me to provide the information for creating reproduction bride's boxes has been a driving force behind this project.

Without the support of my husband, Ray Oxenford, who is responsible for making the actual boxes, as well as assisting with the finishing and waxing, it would not have been possible for this book to become a reality. Likewise, the photographer, Randy Westley, went beyond the call of duty, graciously taking time for our many field trips to capture beautiful photographs of the many antique boxes included within these pages. We are also grateful for his time in working with us to capture each step in the process of making and painting the boxes.

Many antique dealers, private individuals, organizations, and museums graciously gave permission to have their bride's boxes photographed for the book. I wish to acknowledge John and Susan Hoyt, Lancaster County, Pennsylvania; Robert J. Merritt Jr., Douglassville, Pennsylvania; Brian and Sue Hart, Fleetwood, Pennsylvania; Thurston Nichols American Antiques, Breinigsville, Pennsylvania; The Historical Society of Berks County Museum and Library, Reading, Pennsylvania; Tex Johnson Antiques, Adamstown, Pennsylvania (thanks also to Mrs. Johnson and her son, Chris Johnson); Dennis K. Moyer of *The Pennsylvania Farmer*, Zionsville, Pennsylvania; and Landis Valley Museum, Lancaster, Pennsylvania.

Special friends Dr. David Valuska and Dr. Robert Kline have both provided assistance when I needed a German bride's box translated. I am most grateful for their help.

Friend and mentor Louise Diener Stoudt of Wyomissing, Pennsylvania, a second-generation tole and decorative painter, has generously given me a large collection of her old patterns, many of which are bride's boxes. Louise's mother, the late Esther Diener McElroy of Boyertown, Pennsylvania, also was an outstanding painter whose patterns have been a cherished gift. The late James Stoudt, Louise's husband, was a wonderful woodworker among many other fine accomplishments, and he passed on his bride's box forms to us. I am very grateful for their friendships and generosity. I have also been honored to receive patterns from several of Louise's former students, especially the family of the late Ruth Houser of West Lawn, Pennsylvania. My sincere thanks to each of them.

The William Penn Chapter of the Historical Society of Early American Decoration (HSEAD) has many patterns in their collection for rent by the chapter members. The chapter members also painted miniature bride's boxes when they hosted the annual meeting in Wilmington, Delaware, several years ago. They sold kits that included a miniature box along with the patterns. Several designs from those patterns are included in this book. Many thanks to my friend and fellow HSEAD member Ursula Erb for sharing photographs of some of the beautiful bride's boxes she has created. Originally from Germany, Ursula has fashioned many of her designs from originals she found in her homeland. Her bride's boxes were painted with acrylics as well.

To the many clients who have ordered custom-made boxes, I sincerely thank each and every one of you for allowing us to photograph and include these boxes in this book.

Last, but not least, there's my family. In addition to Ray, mentioned above, my daughter Kelly and her husband Matt Simmons, my son Michael and his wife Christine, and my grandchildren Lauren, Erin, and Ryan have always given me encouragement to pursue my artistic talents and follow my dreams.

Introduction

The first bride's box I designed was a project in a class I took from Jackie Shaw of Hagerstown, Maryland, in the fall of 1988, just weeks before our daughter Kelly's wedding. We were given an unpainted box and instructed to decorate it with a floral design of our choice. Already a decorative painter, I began making a stroke floral design. As I was working, I decided to include an inscription around the top edge: "May the gifts of Love and Joy be with you Always." I also included our daughter's and her soon-to-be husband's first names and wedding date. After my return from the class, I gave them the box, and it now serves as the perfect storage place for Kelly's bridal bouquet. From that moment, my interest in creating bride's boxes began. Soon after that, my husband Ray and I purchased a large quantity of imported nested Shaker boxes, which included nine different sizes that I decorated, using the largest size to create designs copied from old bride's boxes. It wasn't until we were invited to the wedding of a friend's daughter that we decided we needed to give a unique handmade gift to the bridal couple, so with that Ray created his first box. I followed by painting a design adapted from a JoSonja Jansen pattern packet. We were excited and pleased with our results. Today, more than two decades later, Ray and I carry on the bride's box tradition.

Little is known about the origins of the highly decorated oval boxes, most commonly known as *bride's boxes*. In Rhineland Europe in the late eighteenth and early nineteenth centuries, these boxes were often part of a bride's dowry and became popular wedding presents. It was also a custom for the groom-to-be to give the bride a box for keeping precious mementos. Or a bride may have used the box for personal items given to her by her family and friends before going into marriage. Often, these boxes, sometimes referred to as "love tokens," were later used to preserve hats, handkerchiefs, documents, candles, trinkets, or sewing supplies. Sometimes, when the first-born arrived, the baptismal clothing, especially the gown used in the ceremony, was preserved in the box for any future siblings.

Many of these early boxes that are found today in Pennsylvania arrived with German-speaking settlers when they left their homeland and journeyed to the New World. Even though the majority of the antique boxes were made in regions of Europe that are today part of Germany or Switzerland, some were made here in America by ancestors of those immigrants who became known as the Pennsylvania Dutch.

Here is an original bride's box from the late 1700s or early 1800s that includes a phrase in German. The translation is "Here give I my hand to bind us together in love." THE HISTORICAL SOCIETY OF BERKS COUNTY MUSEUM AND LIBRARY, READING, PA

These American bride's boxes were mostly made in eastern Pennsylvania, especially in Berks, Lancaster, and Lehigh Counties, where the Pennsylvania Dutch settled.

Most often boxes were made of shaved wood and were known as a *spahn schacteln*, or chip boxes. The old bride's boxes were made of thin solid wood that was steam bent and formed into an elongated oval shape. The wood was then laced together on the sides with leather and the bottom and lid were fastened to the sides with tiny wooden

Pat and Ray Oxenford in their studio.

pegs. Some boxes have not fared well with all the openings and closings during the past two hundred years. The boxes were typically decorated with painted scenes of a man and a woman in formal dress, sometimes by a lake or posed in a portrait-like setting. Other bride's boxes depict elaborate villages or simple pastoral scenes, which may include a young couple. Sometimes the box decorations depicted a man or woman alone, probably the groom or bride. Many had inscriptions printed in German. Some examples of the translation of these sentimental messages were "Be thou mine alone," or "You are my only love." Boxes with scenes painted on the lid were generally painted horizontally while boxes with people on the lid were painted vertically.

Religious motifs and angels were also popular, as well as scenes including dogs or deer. A horse and rider design was considered rare. Other boxes featured floral designs only. Some box designs were painted with elaborate details in bright colors around a lithograph print.

The sides generally had one or two rows of flowers and may have included a top and bottom border of some type, often simple spiral circles or fill-in design. Early boxes were not varnished.

Today, most of the designs I paint on bride's boxes are adaptations of old boxes I have actually seen, photographed, and researched. Sometime I include a combination of several traditional designs in one box. Ray and I are often commissioned for special-order wedding gifts, which are personalized with the bridal couple's name and wedding date on the outside; an inscription to the couple is printed on the inside of the lid.

A reproduction bride's box made by Ray and Pat Oxenford to commemorate their wedding day. The box is based on the original design on page 131.

This book will provide you with all the information you need to create your own bride's boxes. We start with an introduction to all the tools and materials you will need before you start. Then, for those who also want to make the boxes themselves, I've asked Ray to provide step-by-step instructions, from preparing the wood to steam bending and assembling. I then take over with a section on brush strokes and tips for painting, followed by a few projects to get you acquainted with the craft. Then it's up to you. A selection of patterns is included for you to test the skills you've learned. And for further inspiration, galleries of antique and reproduction boxes complete the book. I hope you will find much inspiration and motivation to create your own designs once you see these beautiful creations.

Tools and Materials

Oval Box

You can order premade boxes from a supplier (see page 173), or if you decide you want to construct your own box, step-by-step instructions are provided on page 23. You will need the following tools and materials:

- Cherry, birch, or walnut wood, free of knots or blemishes, 5³/4 x 39 inches for the side band, or body of the box; thickness can range from .100 to .125 inches
- Cherry, birch, or walnut wood, free of knots or blemishes, 1⁹/16 x 39³/4 inches for the lid band; thickness can range from .100 to .125 inches
- 2 pieces of Baltic birch plywood, free of knots or blemishes, for the lid and bottom of the box, each 9 x 14 x ³/8 inches
- Wooden forms (to make, see page 23)
- Copper tacks, #2¹/4, for securing the top and side bands
- Wooden pegs, the size of round toothpicks, to be used for holding the lid and bottom to their respective side bands; use either round toothpicks or wooden skewers
- Band saw, with a 1¹/4-inch carbide blade
- Drill
- Sander
- Drum sander
- Belt sander, with a 1-inch belt
- Dremel tool
- Steam tray
- Portable electric hot plates
- Radial arm saw with Jacobs chuck and a ³/32 drill bit
- Hammer
- Wooden mallet
- Forceps
- Rubber-grip push pad
- Clamps
- Electric branding iron for adding your name to the piece (optional)

Acrylic or Oil Paints

Early bride's boxes were painted in oils, using turpentines, varnishes, and other mediums. Even though I paint in both oils and acrylics, I am using all acrylics to prepare the projects for this book, because I feel they are safer and easier to use. Jo Sonja's Artists' Colours tube paints are my preference for the decorative designs.

If you prefer to work in oils, many different brands are available, such as Grumbacher, Winsor & Newton, and Weber. Be sure to use the proper mediums for oils. A word of caution if you do use oil paints: Make sure you adhere to proper ventilation techniques and consider at least an in-room air purification system for safety reasons.

Mediums

There are specific mediums to mix with your Jo Sonja's Artists' Colours tube paints. Each medium has its own purpose.

- Flow Medium is used to thin your paint to the consistency you need. You can mix it into the paint or keep a small amount in a bottle cap and brush mix it into your paint.
- Gel Retarder is used in the antiquing process.
- Satin Varnish is used as a finish coat to protect your designs.
- Kleister Medium is mixed with your paint when creating faux finishes and other special effects on pictures, such as the transparent look of the lace on the bridal gowns.
- Magic Mix is another medium used to create a transparent effect.
- Stroke and Blending Medium helps with blending as you are pulling your strokes.
- Clear Glaze Medium is great for painting a coat over a dry area to seal the design before painting additional layers on it.

Background Paints

Background surfaces require a larger amount of paint than the decorative design. There are many different brands available: Jo Sonja's Background Colours, Old Village Acrylic Latex Satin Finish paints, and Shades of '76 by Parker Paints. Just a word of caution: Make sure your background paint is compatible with your decorative paint–acrylic with acrylic and oil with oil.

Varnishes

The type of varnish to use depends on the type of background and decorative paint you have applied, acrylic or oil. The particular types shown here are used with oils, but the purpose of this picture is to illustrate how the cans are opened, especially if you brush on your varnish coat. Turn the can upside down and punch a hole along the edge of the bottom with a screw eye inserted. To release varnish, remove the screw eye and turn the can over for the varnish to flow freely from the can. This procedure prevents a skin from forming on your varnish.

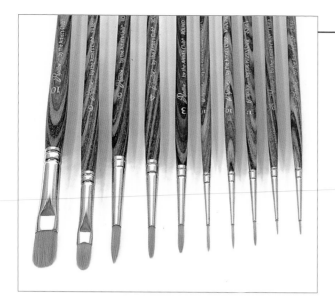

Brushes

Round and filbert brushes are required for creating details in flowers, the bride's gown, and other smaller objects within the design,

Shader or flat brushes (left) of various sizes are used for the geometric side borders, the bands on the lids, and banner areas where the names and date are placed.

Striping brushes (right) are used for the stripe details around the box lid and side.

A 1-inch brush or a foam brush is used to paint the background surfaces.

Brush Holder

Since many different brushes are used for a project, this handy gadget prevents them from rolling around. It is actually a 1-inch dowel rod cut in half with indentations created by a disc sander.

Water Basin

When using acrylic paint, the brushes are cleaned with water. Usually brushes are cleaned in a water basin or bucket after the use of each individual color and before another color is incorporated into the brush. The exception is when the design calls for the "dirty-brush technique," when you do not clean your brush after each color's use. A word about the water temperature: Always use cool to cold water, never hot water, to clean your brushes. Hot water will set the paint in the bristles and make it more difficult to remove.

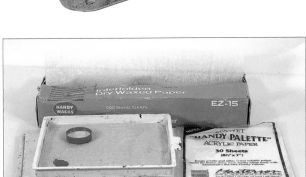

Paint Box

A paint box is storage space for paint you will be using for the decorative process. Paint boxes usually come with a thin piece of foam included, although you can prepare one by folding several layers of shop towels and cutting them to the size of the box. Wet the prepared towels or foam thoroughly, wring out the excess water, and place a sheet of dry deli wrap around the prepared towels. Doing this helps keep your paint pliable longer. Sta-Wet Acrylic Pallet Paper, made to fit the paint box, is also available.

Spray Bottle

A spray bottle is handy to occasionally spray or mist your paints to keep them pliable and workable longer.

Brush Cleaner

Periodically throughout the painting process, and especially at the end of a painting session, brushes need to be thoroughly cleaned. Apply brush cleaner soap to the bristles, work it into the bristles with your fingers, and brush the bristles back and forth over a pick board to clean. You may also want to purchase a brush-cleaning brush to use over the bristles to assist in removing paint from the bristles.

Pallet Knives

Various sizes and styles of pallet knives are available for mixing paint colors.

Pallet

A paper pallet or a waxed paper pallet are used for mixing paint and especially for dressing your brush properly. To dress, load by tipping your brush and picking up paint on its side, and brush back and forth on the pallet to work the paint into the bristles.

Jars and Lids

Jars of various sizes are good for keeping workable amounts of paint mediums, especially when you purchase large-quantity containers. Jars are also great when you are working on a large project and need to keep a special background color mixture handy, especially for any touch-up spots. Use jar lids or recycled communion cups for holding special mixtures as you paint. Use larger lids to cover smaller lids holding your special mixture paints during your work session.

Paint Strainer (metal can, small paper cup, nylon stocking, and rubber band)

If you need to mix a quantity of paint, or even your varnish, it is best to strain the paint to ensure that it is free of dust or dirt. Use a recycled tomato paste can that you have placed painter's tape around the top opening, insert a small paper cup into the can, cut pieces of recycled nylon stocking to place over the paper cup, secure with a rubber band, and you have a paint strainer.

Bridges

If you are uneasy about getting your wrist or hand into a freshly painted area of your project, painting bridges aid in keeping your hand elevated. There are commercial plastic versions available, or you can make your own out of wood.

Paint Block

To help paint straight lines, such as the stripes across the bottom of the box lid where the name and date are placed, use either blue painter's tape or Frogtape. Make sure any previous paint is thoroughly dry. Carefully pull the tape off once your newly painted area is dry to the touch.

Pick Board

Pick boards are great for drying your projects, especially in the base-coating process.

Painter Pyramids

A relatively new item to elevate your project while base coating is the painter pyramid. Please note that if you are using a soft wood, do not press down on the pyramids while painting; the point underneath may leave a mark.

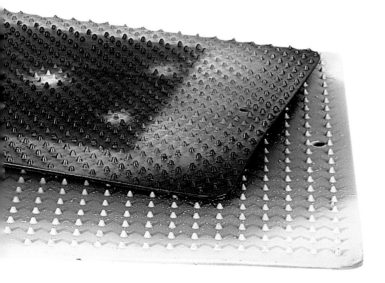

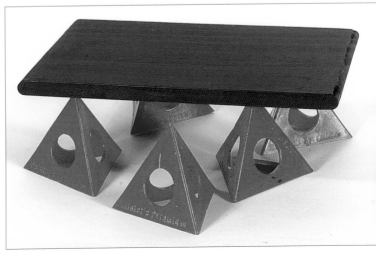

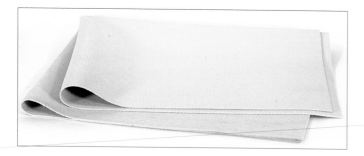

Sanding Foam Cloth and Splat Mat

A woodworker's sanding foam cloth works well on the painting table to cushion the object being decorated. Also a Splat Mat placed over the sanding foam cloth aids in quick cleanup in case any paint gets on the table. At times, I use two Splat Mats, side-by-side, if it is a large object that is being decorated. They are reusable and clean up easily; just wipe them with a damp cloth and the paint is gone.

Waste Bags

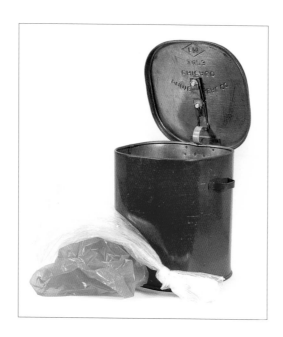

Tape a bag to the side of your painting table to dispose of any potentially hazardous cloth or paper towels. At the end of each painting session, squeeze out all the air from the bag and tightly tie or knot the top. Dispose of the bag in a metal trash container with a tight-fitting lid or a hazardous waste container. Do not take chances, especially when working with oils and turps; they are potentially combustible. For my waste bags, I recycle the plastic sleeves from newspapers.

Drawing Board

For ease in the designing process a portable desk-top drawing board is ideal.

Light Box

If you do a lot of designing, a light box is a good investment. It is great for tracing.

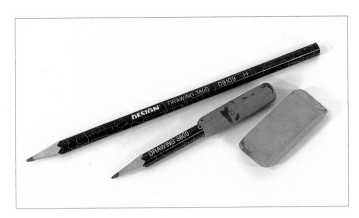

Pencil And Eraser

When designing patterns it is preferable to use a hard-lead drawing pencil. Keep a Pink Pearl Eraser nearby.

Pastel Chalk Pencils

Chalk pencils in both white and gray are great for marking bands and borders directly on the painting surface.

Rulers and Measuring Tape

Various rulers and tape measures are used when creating a design on the box:
- 6-inch flexible steel ruler
- 18-inch flexible steel ruler
- Transparent plastic T-square
- Transparent rulers of various sizes
- 36-inch measuring tape
- Small retractable measuring tape
- 24-inch flexible ruler

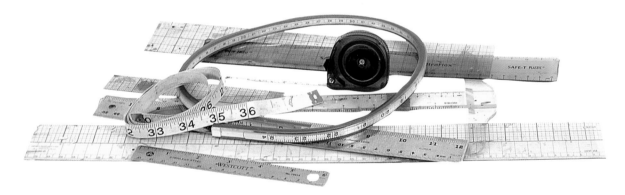

Transfer Paper

Once the design is perfected, use Saral transfer paper to copy the design to the painting surface.

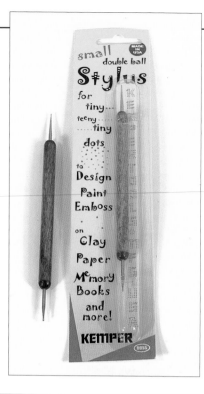

Stylus

Trace the design onto the painting surface with a stylus.

Weights

Dressmaker's weights are useful for holding the pattern in place on a wood surface.

Sheet Tin and Magnets

Pieces of sheet tin in various sizes are great for keeping paper secure when creating patterns. Cover the edges of the tin with tape to prevent cuts to your fingers. Then use small magnets to secure your paper in place on the tin.

Pens and Markers

When preparing patterns, tracing a pattern, or even signing your name to an item, technical pens are a good choice. Rapidograph by Koh-i-Noor is my first choice. Sharpie also makes a good fine-point, felt-tip marker–permanent black ink, of course. A Rapidograph pen occasionally will become clogged. Keep a small jar of Windex or glass cleaner nearby for quickly cleaning a pen point. Just dip your pen tip in.

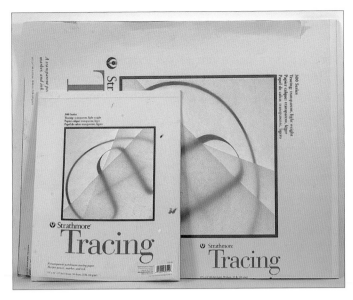

Tracing Paper

Tracing paper comes in many sizes. It is good to have several sizes of tablets available.

Vellum

Vellum is a heavyweight surface that is great for practice painting your design or for making a permanent painted pattern.

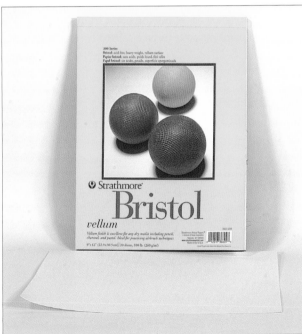

Waterproof Sandpaper and Dishwashing Liquid

A vital part of a great finished product is sanding. You will use various grits of sandpaper. Cut sheets of 600-grit, 1,200-grit, and 1,500-grit sandpaper into small squares, rounding the corners so you do not jab into the box while you are sanding it. In a small plastic container, mix about $1/2$ inch of water with a drop or so of Palmolive or other dish liquid. You will soak the sandpaper in the soapy water for several minutes prior to sanding. The wet sandpaper may need to be dipped again several times during a sanding procedure. Use an old towel to cushion the sanding work surface. When you have finished sanding make sure you thoroughly clean off the sanding slurry from your project. It is helpful to have a dedicated sanding area near a sink and water.

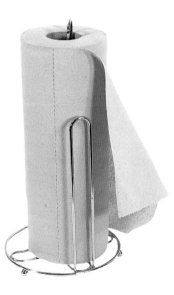

Shop Towels

Shop towels are good for cleaning the project after wet sanding. Often you will need to dampen a shop towel and wipe the surface, followed by using a dry shop towel to dry the project thoroughly before proceeding.

Sanding Pads

Sanding pads of various grits are also good for sanding. Cut the larger pieces into smaller sizes, so you have better control when sanding and are able to get into the hard-to-reach areas.

Tack Cloth

When you are finished sanding, use a tack cloth to thoroughly wipe over the entire surface to remove any remaining sanding dust. This is an extremely important step to eliminate any dust particles on the painting surface.

Wet Naps

Wet naps are great for removing paint from your hands or unwanted paint on your surface caused by an error.

Making the Box

B efore a bride's box can be painted, it has to be created. You can buy unpainted boxes from craftsmen (see page 173), but if you wish to make your own boxes, my husband Ray will demonstrate the process in this chapter. For the projects in this book, you will need two sizes of boxes.

To begin, you will need to make several different *forms* as guides for shaping the thin, steamed wood of the boxes. Ray has built this form for the smaller of the two different-sized boxes. The form should be solid and can be made from several pieces of scrap wood glued together, rough cut to shape, and then sanded to get the exact size; notice in the photo the visible lines where the wood has been glued together and the markings that indicate where to start and end the wrap. The forms must be extremely smooth and precise in size. You will make the lids after you form the body of the box.

You will also need two shapers or formers to make each size box. They are made from a piece of 3/4-inch pine or plywood. They should be slightly oversized with a 12-degree bevel and should be inserted into each end of the box band while it is drying so that the band holds its shape. For easy insertion and removal, two holes should be drilled into each shaper.

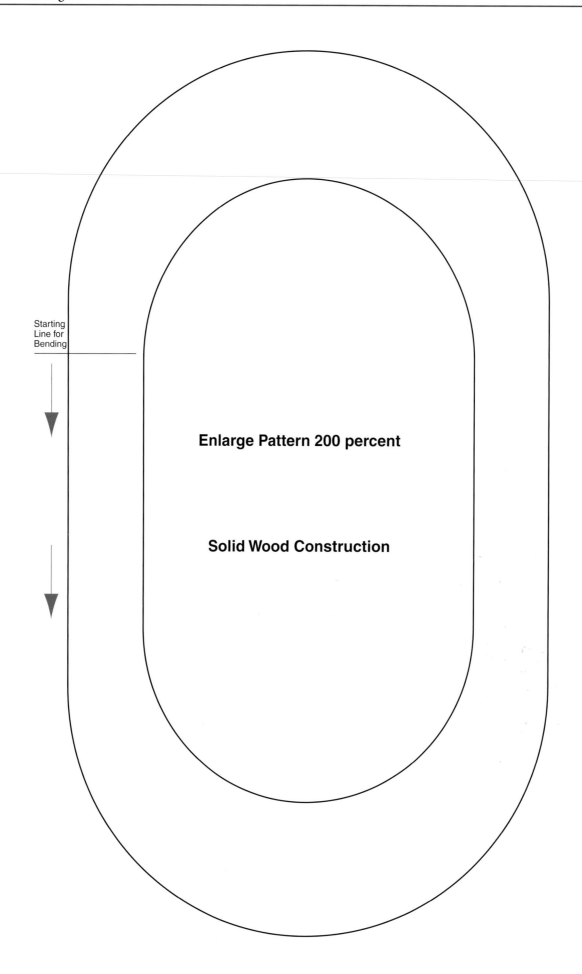

Starting
Line for
Bending

Enlarge Pattern 200 percent

Solid Wood Construction

On the facing page is a pattern to make the form for the small box. The particular piece of wood needed for the body of this box is $5^3/4$ x 39 inches. It should be free of blemishes or knots. Its lid band will measure $1^9/16$ x $39^3/4$.

Here is the pattern for the large box form. The measurements of the wood for the body are $5^3/4$ x 55 inches. The lid band will be $1^9/16$ x $56^3/4$.

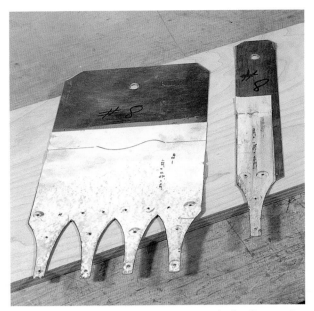

Next, you will need templates to mark the fingers that will attach the two ends of the bands of wood for the body and lid of the box. Make them from tin from the patterns provided on the next page.

Select your piece of wood. We recommend cherry, birch, or walnut that is free of knots or blemishes. Using a band saw with a $1^1/4$-inch carbide blade, cut the wood to the desired thickness of $5/32$ inch. Cut the wood to length and width required.

Then use a surface sander to surface the wood to a range of between .100 and .125 thickness.

At one end of the wood for the box body, mark the finger positions.

Here are the templates for the fingers. Each box has two different pieces, one for the body band and another for the lid band. The patterns are used for both box sizes, but the length will be longer for the larger box, as specified on page 25.

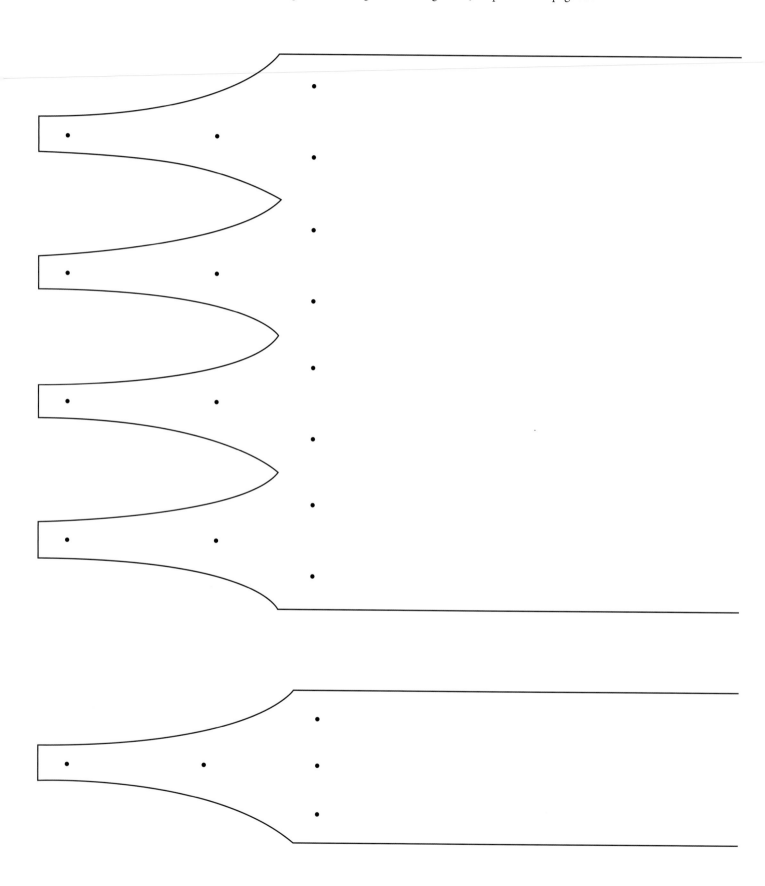

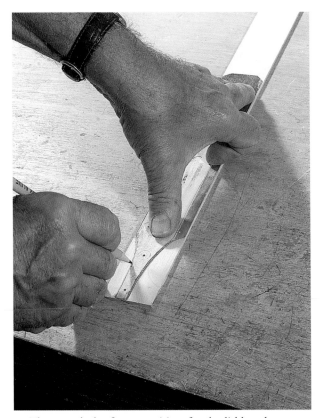

Then mark the finger position for the lid band.

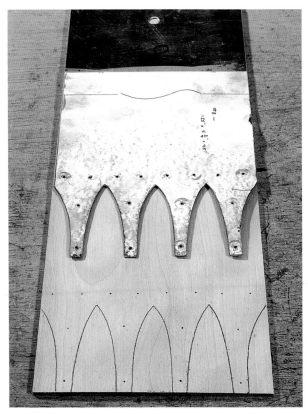

This is how the body band appears once the fingers and tack holes have been marked.

Using an awl, mark the location on the body band for the placement of the copper tacks that will secure the sides together. Do the same for the lid piece.

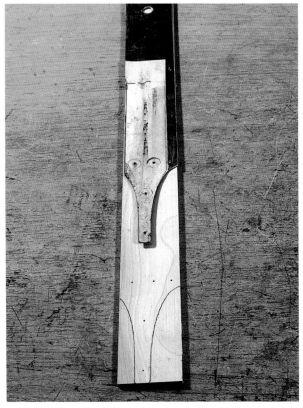

This is how the lid band appears once the markings are noted.

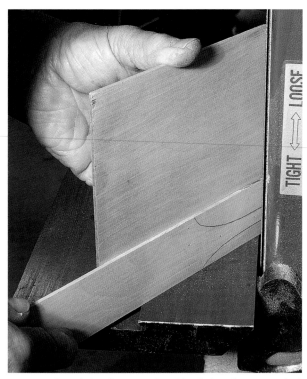

Next, bevel the finger ends of both bands using a belt sander.

The beveled edge of the fingers should look like this. Now, using a drill with a 1/16-inch drill bit, make the holes for the tacks on both band pieces. When making multiple boxes of the same size, secure several like-size box bands together and drill the holes at the same time.

The size indicated for the holes might seem too large, but when the wood is heated later, it will expand and the holes will become smaller.

Using a 1/4-inch fine-tooth blade on the band saw, begin to cut out the fingers of the body.

Proceed to cut out the finger for the lid band.

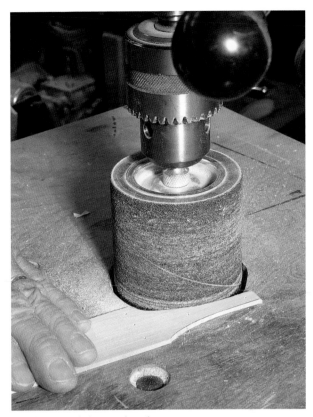

Then sand the top band.

Now use the drum sander to sand the outer edges of the fingers for a nice, graceful curve.

Next, use a belt sander with a 1-inch-wide belt to sand the inner sides of the fingers.

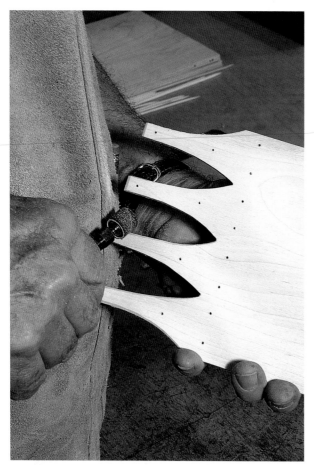

Then, using a Dremel tool fitted with a small sanding disc, bevel the edges of the fingers.

Here is how the fingers should look after sanding and beveling.

Now is the time to bevel the overlap on the opposite end of the fingers on the side band. Make a mark on the wood to note the depth of 1¹/₄ inches from the end, which allows for the feathering to be done on the sander.

Then bevel it down.

Note the thickness of the sides and how it tapers down to a very thin sliver of wood at the end. This allows for a nice overlap.

The wood is ready to be steamed so that it can be bent. Steam trays are available in copper and stainless steel; with either type, two portable electric hot plates, each with two burners, are required to properly heat the water. Place the prepared bands in the steamer and allow them to steam for approximately twenty minutes, or until the wood is pliable enough to bend around the form without splitting.

Using a forceps, remove the bands from the hot water bath.

Quickly place the body band around the form. It's convenient to have someone help you with this part. Here, Ray holds the inside end in place with a piece of wood, so that it doesn't split, while I follow along holding a rubber-grip push pad with handle against the wood also to keep it from splitting.

Once the wood is completely around the form, it is very important to keep the fingers down and in place with the aid of the rubber-grip push pad. When the wood is bent to shape, put a light pencil mark at the overlap position of each finger.

Quickly remove the wood from the form and reform it again, clamping it in place with a piece of wood over the fingers. Important: If you do not hold all the fingers down at the same time, the wood has a tendency to split between the fingers and you must begin again with another piece of wood.

Now with the wood band clamped together, place it over an anvil or other hard surface. Put the #2¼ copper tacks in the pre-drilled holes and nail them in place. The tacks will penetrate both thicknesses of wood and will actually bend over underneath when they make contact with the anvil. This prevents the tacks from becoming loose and falling out.

The last tacks are inserted in the very ends of the fingers.

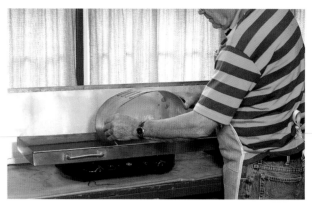

Next, place the box back into the hot water bath, rotating it until it is dampened.

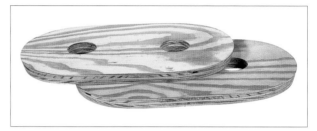

Insert the two shapers, which have a 12-degree level, into the top and bottom of the box.

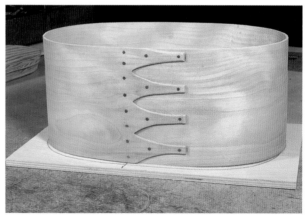

It is now time to make a bottom and top. Ray recommends Baltic birch plywood that is free of knots and blemishes for the tops and bottoms of the boxes. Baltic birch plywood is very stable with very little shrinkage. Use a pencil to trace the inside of the box onto the wood. Notice the mark on the bottom just below the line of copper tacks; it is important when inserting the bottom to realign the mark with the tacks so that the box maintains its oval shape.

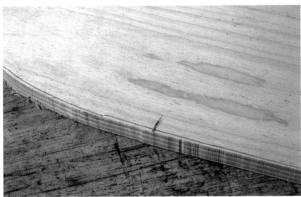

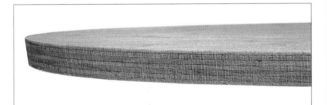

Cut the bottom out and sand to a 4-degree inward bevel, which allows you to get a good snug fit.

The bottom is now ready to be inserted. Use a wooden mallet to lightly tap it into place. Be careful not to hit it too hard or you may split the side band.

When the bottom is dry, you can make the band for the lid. Steam the lid band in the hot water bath for approximately twenty minutes, until it is pliable.

Follow the same procedure for bending the lid band as you did for the body of the box.

Mark the finger overlap with a pencil line, except this time allow approximately 1/8 to 3/16 inch larger to allow for the proper lid clearance.

Then proceed to nail the band together using the #21/4 copper tacks.

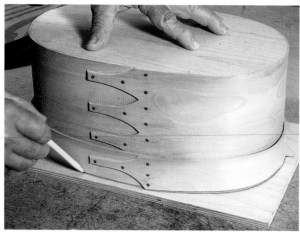

Now you will prepare the lid. This procedure is exactly the same as the box bottom. Use a pencil to trace the outside of the box onto the wood so you do not lose the original contour shape of the lid. Carefully sand to fit properly.

Make the pencil mark for alignment. Cut the lid out and sand to a 4-degree inward bevel.

When the lid is fit properly, tap it into place with the wooden mallet.

Here is the lid at this point.

Now you will make holes for inserting the wooden pegs or skewers that will secure the bands to the top and bottom. Start with the body of the box. Use a Jacobs chuck mounted on the accessory end of the motor of a radial arm saw. When using this saw, you will need to elevate the box and lid approximately three inches off the table. This will allow you to drill a perfect horizontal hole to insert the pegs. With a 3/32 drill bit, proceed to make holes about every 4 inches around the box.

Do the same thing for the lid.

Use the belt sander to smooth the pegs against the box and lid.

Insert wooden pegs or skewers into the pre-drilled holes, using a drop of glue.

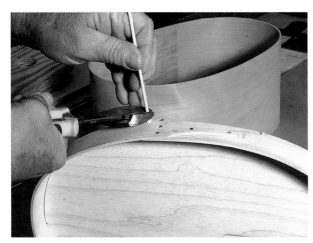

Next cut off the excess peg.

Now sand the box and lid with the floppy disc sander.

And lastly, sign the piece with an electric branding iron.

Here is the completed box.

Basic Painting Skills

Now that you have a box, you are ready to begin painting. Here are some of the basic skills for decorative painting that you will want to develop as you move on to the projects in this book.

Adding the Background Color

You will begin by preparing the background surface, starting with the lid. Place a woodworker's mat on the table, with two Splat Mats on top. Elevate the lid on four stacks of painter's pyramids to enable ease in painting the outside surface. In this case, two different colors were mixed together for the background color of the large lid and all-purpose sealer was added for the first coat of paint. Paint a base coat on both the lid and box body.

Apply the prepared paint with a foam brush, painting the top in elongated strokes.

It is best to brush in the same back and forth direction, following the grain of the wood versus going crosswise. Allow the paint to dry thoroughly and then wet sand. Clean the slurry with a damp shop towel and dry thoroughly. Repeat a second coat of base color, adding Clear Glaze medium to the mixture. Again dry thoroughly. Lightly sand again, clean, and dry. If you are pleased with the coverage of your basecoat, allow the surface to dry completely before proceeding with the decorating.

Basic Brush Strokes

A few basic brush strokes are used in decorating a bride's box. If you are a beginning painter, spend time practicing the strokes before you start a project. Use scraps of Bristol board or gift-box cardboard for practice. You may want to place tracing paper over the brush strokes in the book and paint over them to get the feel of the strokes.

Tips for Painting

Here are some suggestions to help make designing and painting easier for you.

- Long fingernails and the decorative painter do not go well together. Fingernails tend to get in the way, oftentimes clicking or rubbing against the surface of the object you are trying to decorate, which could scratch or mar the surface before it is dry or cured.

- Avoid wearing clothing that is fuzzy or sheds lint easily, such as a sweater, to keep a clean surface.

- When painting the background surface, you may wish to wear disposable rubber gloves to keep paint off your hands. And, if you have sensitive skin, you may also want to wear disposable rubber gloves when wet sanding.

- If you have long hair, it is best to tie it back into a ponytail to prevent it from dragging through the freshly painted surface as you look down onto your project to work.

- An apron is helpful for keeping paint off your clothing.

Right Comma Stroke

Begin with a number 6 round brush and Bristol board to make the right comma stroke. Think of an imaginary clock face with the position of 12 at the top, 3 on the right, 6 at the bottom, and 9 on the left.

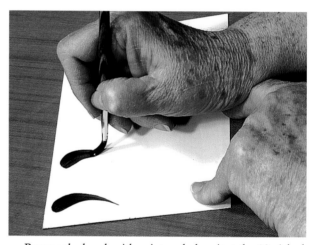

Prepare the brush with paint and place it at the 12 o'clock position. Gently press the brush to spread the bristles and begin pulling it toward the 3 o'clock position, gradually lifting as you are pulling.

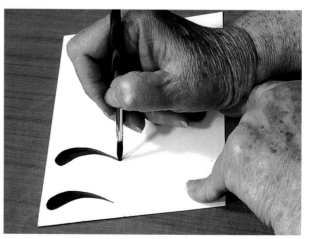

By the time you reach the 6 o'clock position, your brush should be up on the tip of the bristles and the tail of the stroke to a fine line.

Left Comma Stroke

To reverse the comma stroke, turn the object a quarter turn to the left, so that the stroke will be pulled beginning at the 9 o'clock position, passing through the 6 o'clock position, and ending at the 3 o'clock position.

Rotating the object you are decorating as you pull the right comma or left comma stroke gives you a good mirror image.

Teardrop Stroke

The teardrop stroke is a straight-line stroke pulled from 12 o'clock to 6 o'clock.

Begin at the 12 position, press and spread the bristles of the brush, and pull straight downward.

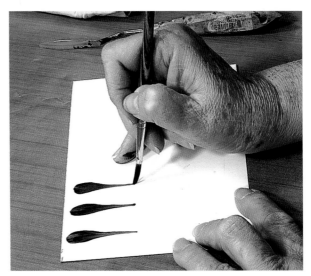

Gently lift the brush as you come to a fine point.

Elongated S Stroke

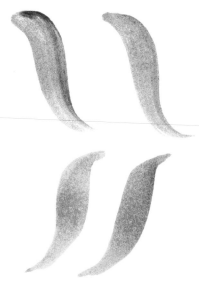

An elongated S stroke is used for tulip designs on the sides of the box. Depending on the design size you want, you may want to increase to the number 8 brush.

Lightly rest the brush on its tip and pull slightly to the right.

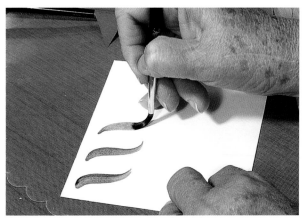

Increase the pressure as you change direction slightly to the left.

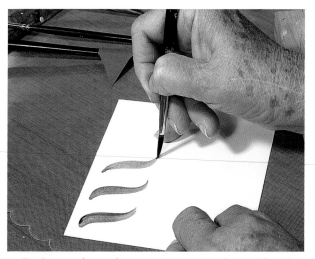

Begin to release the pressure as you change direction again and end on the right.

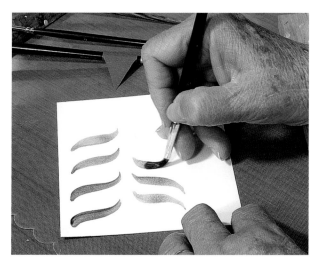

For the left elongated S, pull slightly to the left and increase pressure as you change direction to the right.

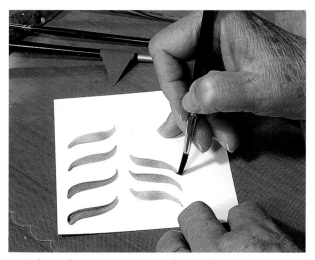

Release the pressure as you change direction again and end to the left.

Circle

Small, round circles are made with a flat number 6 or 8 brush. To demonstrate the movement in the pictures, I have attached a tape flag to the top of the brush handle.

Keep the brush perpendicular to the work surface.

Press down, turning the brush a full 360 degrees, or a full circle. Notice that I have overextended my index finger inward, holding the brush between thumb and index finger, and twirled the brush to the right to make a full circle. Look at the tape flag to see how the brush rotates.

Striping

Striping is used frequently around the top edge of the lid and sometimes around the bottom edge of the side. A striping brush works well. The amount of pressure applied to the brush bristles determines how thick or thin the stripe line will be.

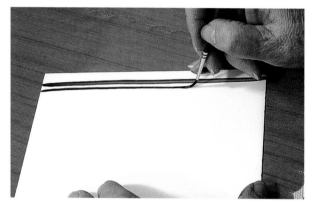

Place the brush bristles parallel with the edge of the surface. As you pull the stripe, keep your little finger along the edge of the surface as a guide to make the stripe as straight as possible.

Fine Details

Fine details are frequently made on the bride's boxes using a 10/0 script brush.

Loops

Some details consist of a stroke resembling a connected series of the cursive letter "e."

Thin Comma Strokes

Or you may need to make thinner comma strokes. They are executed the same as the thicker versions on page 38.

Spirals

Spirals, or curlicues, are frequently seen as background or fill-in strokes, especially on black or dark-background bride's boxes. Begin in the center and move the brush in a circular outward motion. Vary the size of these so that some are larger than others. This is a good practice stroke for loosening up and relaxing as you begin a painting session.

Templates

Sides of bride's boxes, especially those with dark backgrounds, have large flowers with overstroke details. Recycled rack cards or advertising cards are good for making reusable templates or patterns that aid in making consistent-shape flowers. Here are two different sets of suggested floral designs for the side of the bride's box. Enlarge or decrease the designs depending on the size of your box.

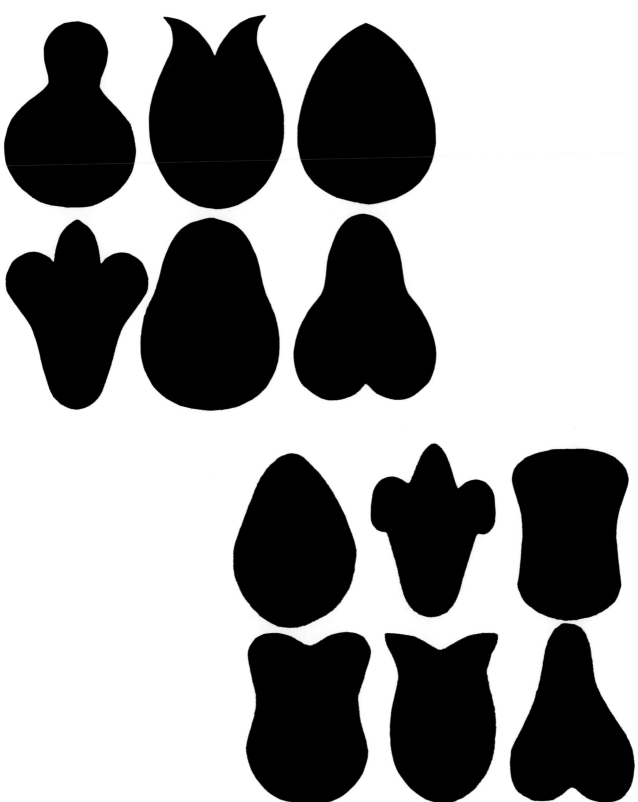

Letters

Here is the alphabet in the Old German text, which was commonly used on traditional bride's boxes. Notice that Q and W are not in the sequence; this is because they did not exist in the German alphabet. They are included at the end of each set, however, if you wish to use them. It is important to remember that you will be turning your box or lid to pull the letters properly; it cannot be done in one continuous stroke.

Review the alphabet with the arrows to show the sequence you should pull the strokes for each section of each letter. For smaller-sized letters, adjust your brush accordingly. You can use a number 3 round brush for this size, but you may want to use a fine liner brush for the thinner lines rather than attempting a light pressure on the tip of the bristles of the number 3. If necessary, use a bridge to elevate your hand and wrist off the painting surface.

abcdefghijklmno

prstuvxyz

qw

abcdefghijklmnoprs

tuvxyzqw

1 2 3 4 5 6 7 8 9

0 , . ♥

1 2 3 4 5 6 7 8 9

0 , . ♥

Antiquing

When you have finished painting your bride's box, you may want to give it an antique appearance. To antique the box, follow these steps for the lid, bottom, and sides.

- Starting with the lid, use the tack cloth to remove any dust from the box.

- Apply a coat of Gel Retarder to the surface as evenly as possible with a sponge brush.

- Now, with a sponge or bristle brush, apply an even coat of the antique paint. Burnt Umber works well for this effect.

- Next, with a shop towel folded into a pad, gently remove the excess paint until you have the desired amount of antiquing for your project. You can also use a mop brush, gently and lightly brushing back and forth over the surface to blend the antiquing.

- If you need to lighten up any areas, remove more antiquing with the shop towel or mop brush until you have achieved your desired effect. A word of caution: Try to refrain from touching the painted surface you are antiquing to avoid leaving your fingerprints.

- Let the entire box dry overnight. A quick method of drying is with a hand-held hair dryer, but be careful to hold the dryer at a safe distance from your painting surface.

- After drying, check the surface for any dust or bristles, especially if using the mop brush.

- Proceed with the final varnish coats. Remember to wet sand and dry thoroughly between coats.

Facial features on bride's boxes were very primitive. They did not have much detail, and typically did not have happy expressions. Here are the basic steps for painting faces.

Begin with Skin Tone Base for the oval shape of the face. The arrows indicate the direction you should pull the strokes.

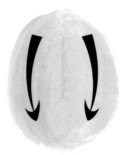

Mark the face with a gray chalk pencil in sections for placement of the eyes, nose, and mouth. The center line indicates that the man will be looking to his left, or towards the lady. If using this method on your design, use a white chalk pencil that can be erased easily once the paint is dry.

Begin to paint in the white for eyes in tiny football shapes; many old designs used small circles for the eyes, so you might want to consider that option. Remember to turn your work and pull the strokes from the center out. The nose is a short, quick comma stroke, pulled from the bottom to the top, so turn your face upside down to make it. Use two short strokes of Burnt Sienna to create the mouth. Also, make a fine outline of Burnt Sienna with the 10/0 liner or script brush around the edge of the face, making the detail slightly heavier on the left side.

Now, you will paint in the irises of the eyes. I used Prussian Blue Hue here, although you can also use shades of brown. Make very small circles. Also dust the cheek area with highlights of Napthol Red Light or a red of your choice.

Add a few details of thin white strokes across the forehead and chin area. Make a tiny white dot for the eye highlights. For each eyebrow, done here in Burnt Sienna, turn your work to the proper position and pull a comma stroke from the center out. You may want to define the nose a little more by pulling a fine line detail in Burnt Sienna. Add the hairstyle of your choice.

Here are additional examples of expressions, hairstyles, and even hats, as well as one profile. Often, the man was portrayed in a side profile looking at his bride.

Mark the face with a gray chalk pencil in sections for placement of the eyes, nose, and mouth, as you did for the man, except the lady will be looking to her right, towards the man.

For the lady, extend the Skin Tone Base to the upper chest area; most brides are portrayed in gowns with low necklines. Here again, the arrows indicate the direction you should pull the strokes. Begin painting the oval for the face and then move to the neck and upper chest area with strokes flowing left and right

Paint the whites of the eyes, and then make the white comma stroke for the nose. You may want to mix Napthol Red Light with Burnt Sienna for the two strokes that make the lady's mouth. To give some details to the lady's neckline with thin Burnt Sienna, add a few strokes to her left side, and a few strokes of a lighter shade of skin tone (brush-mix a little white into your skin tone) to highlight her right side.

Add the irises in shades of either blue or brown, and add the tiny white highlight dot. You may also want to define the nose with a fine line of Burnt Sienna. Highlight the cheeks with a dusting of Napthol Red Light. Most brides wore a transparent or lace cap; I prefer to paint in the hair first, however, so that it can be seen under the cap.

To add a cap, use Kleister Medium with White; however, for the purpose of visibility, I have used Yellow Oxide and White mixed with Kleister. The transparent paint represents the fine lace cap. You may want to add a few dangly curls at the position of the lady's ears.

Projects

D etailed directions are provided for the first project; however, it is assumed you will follow through with these steps on the following projects, and these instructions will not be repeated. The preparation of your box prior to painting, including sanding and wet sanding between base coats, cleaning the slurry from wet sanding, and the use of the tack cloth are all very important steps in the process of decorative painting. If you do not prepare your box properly, which includes sanding and cleaning your work during the painting process, no matter how great your decorative painting, the item will not have a good appearance. Preparation during the decorative process is extremely important; do not take chances with shortcuts.

PROJECT 1
Continental Floral Decoration
page 52

PROJECT 2
Pennsylvania Gentleman
page 62

PROJECT 3
Angel
page 67

The first project is an adaptation of a small bride's box that was recently sold at Pook & Pook, an auction house in Downingtown, Pennsylvania. I took a picture of it, and this design was created from that picture.

• The first step is to sand the box and lid. If there are any blemishes that require wood filler, fill those spots, sand again, and use a tack cloth to remove any dust.

• Paint the box and lid black with a foam brush. See "Adding the Background Color" on page 37 for complete instructions. Traditionally, the outside bottom of the box was not painted; you may prefer, however, to cover all surfaces.

• Apply a minimum of two coats of the black basecoat, wet-sanding between coats.

• Allow the basecoats to dry thoroughly before proceeding to the decorating process.

Here is the design for the lid. Enlarge or reduce it as needed to fit your box.

Begin by making a tracing paper pattern to the exact size of your box. Then, using Saral paper, a stylus, and dress-maker's weights to hold the pattern in place, trace only the main parts of the design–for this box, that means the outline of the large flower and the ovals and stem placements around it. Do not trace any other detail lines.

After the design is traced, use the tack cloth to remove any dust from the Saral paper.

- Prepare your paint. I used the following JoSonja's Artists' Colours tube paints for this project:

    Warm White
    Vermilion
    Indian Red Oxide
    Mix of Prussian Blue Hue and Warm White
    Green Oxide added to the blue for a greenish-blue
        mixture for stems

- Depending on the paint consistency, you may want to add Flow Medium to your paint, being cautious not to add too much; I prefer to tip my brush into the Flow Medium versus adding it to the paint mix.

Using a number 3, 4, or 5 brush (whichever you are comfortable with), begin painting the flower, following the photograph of the finished box at the beginning of this chapter.

Paint the lower two ball flowers white and the upper two ball flowers vermilion. Create the ball flowers by filling in the lines with a series of comma strokes (see page 38).

Paint the petals of the large flower with a mixture of Prussian Blue hue and Warm White, adding some White on the brush.

All the flowers are made using a combination of right and left comma strokes and teardrop strokes. Remember to turn your work as required to pull the strokes properly. See page 44.

Notice the paint is not blended completely, but has streaks of white.

Now, paint the stem and leaves with a mixture of Prussian Blue hue and Green Oxide, working from the top down.

Notice some leaves begin with a point instead of a rounded end. This stroke is pulled just like a comma stroke, except you do not place the pressure on the bristles; just tip the brush and begin pulling as you apply pressure, continuing the same as the comma stroke.

You may also need to apply another coat of paint to these areas before doing the details.

After completing one side of leaves, proceed to the other side, starting again from the top down.

Next, paint the band around the top edge using a number 20 shader brush and the Indian Red Oxide paint.

If necessary, use the painting bridge so that you do not get your hand into the wet paint.

While you are waiting for the design to thoroughly dry, carefully begin to mark off the band area on the bottom edge of the lid band. The top and bottom borders should each be one inch. Use a white or gray chalk pencil for this procedure.

Once the lid is marked, use a flexible ruler as a guide to connect the marks.

Also mark the bottom border area.

Then put the lid on the box and mark the depth of the lid side drop.

Decide which flowers you prefer for the side of the box and determine how many you will need to have. Then make templates of each; see page 43. A dressmaker's measuring tape works well for determining the distance between each flower. Now, trace the desired flower templates, evenly spaced around the side of the box.

Brush strokes should follow the lines of each flower; this tulip begins with an oval bowl at the top.

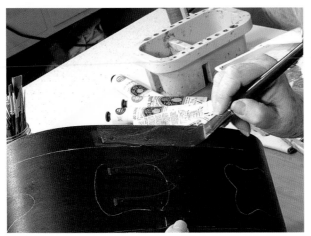

Using the number 20 shader brush, paint the bands around the top edge of the lid side and the bottom side edge with Indian Red Oxide. If two coats are needed for good coverage of these bands, lightly sand them, clean with the tack cloth, and paint a second coat.

Then make strokes to indicate the flower petal line. After finishing the first blue flower, pass by the next two flower outlines and paint the third one blue in the same manner.

Now you are ready to paint in the flowers on the sides. In the example, there are six flowers: two blue, two white, and two vermilion. Use a round brush—something between number 4 and number 6, depending on which you are most comfortable using.

Now, clean the brush and use Warm White paint for the two flower outlines to the right of each of the blue flowers.

Then, clean the brush again and paint the remaining two flowers in Vermilion.

When the flowers are all based in, use the green mixture on a round number 4 or 5 brush. Pull a teardrop stroke for the stem of each flower.

Then, with the same green mixture and round brush, make four leaves on each stem.

While the box dries, paint the small circles at random intervals with Indian Red Oxide on the lid, using a number 6 or 8 flat or shader brush.

Here is what the lid will look like at this point.

Then paint the circles on the side of the box.

Follow the photo of the finished lid for making the following details:

- Place a white dot in the center of each red ball.
- Then make white balls randomly on the black background.
- Now, check the pattern for the overstroke details on the flower petals, buds, stem, and leaves. You will be doing these in freehand instead of marking lines.
- Using a 10/0 or 18/0 script brush with Yellow Oxide paint brush-mixed with Flow Medium, add the yellow line details to the blue petals, white and vermilion buds, and green stem and leaves.
- Clean the brush before adding the white details to the vermilion buds.
- Using the striper brush and white paint, make a fine-line oval border separating the black and Indian Red Oxide border.
- Clean the brush and with Yellow Oxide pull an oval border about the middle of the Indian Red Oxide border.
- Outside of the yellow strip are evenly placed fine-line comma strokes. Using a 1 or 2 liner brush, pull these strokes around the outside edge. If you are not comfortable freehanding these strokes, use your dressmaker's measuring tape and make a dot or indication with the chalk pencil as to the length of the strokes so that they are evenly spaced.

Now follow the photo to complete the details on the side of the box.

- The blue and vermilion flowers both have white details, while the white flower and the leaves have Yellow Oxide details.
- Mark both the top and bottom band of the side and stripe and make comma strokes in the same manner as the lid band. Allow the decorations to dry thoroughly.

Finish the box following these directions:

- Clean up any excess chalk markings with a Pink Pearl eraser, and then use a tack cloth to remove any dust.
- Using a 1 1/2-inch brush or foam brush, apply a coat of varnish to the box and lid, and then let them dry thoroughly.
- Next, lightly wet sand both parts, clean them, and let them dry.
- Although the insides of bride's boxes were left bare, I prefer to follow through and paint them, often creating a faux finish. You might want to paint the interior a complementary color, stain it, or even sponge paint it. Another possibility would be to create a fabric interior with a complementary calico material. You decide what you would prefer to do.
- At this point decide if you want to give the box an antique effect (see page 47).
- If you would rather not antique the box, apply two more coats of varnish, wet sanding and drying between coats. Remember it is very important to allow the box to thoroughly dry between coats.
- Finish with a coat of wax of your choice. Waxing is optional.

PROJECT 2: *Pennsylvania Gentleman*

Early bride's boxes often portrayed figures of men and women and were usually made and decorated in regions that make up present-day Germany and Switzerland. This design, however, is thought to have originated in Pennsylvania. The original box measured 15 inches long, 11 inches wide and 5½ inches deep. The design adapts well to the #6 Shaker box, but can be easily increased or decreased to fit other sizes.

Here is the pattern for the lid. Determine which size box you want to use, and enlarge or reduce the size of the pattern to fit accordingly.

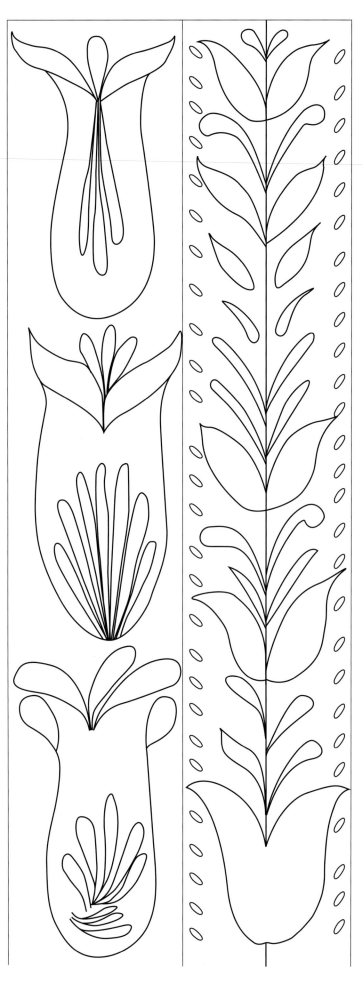

Here is the pattern for the side of the box. You will need to adjust the size accordingly and then repeat the pattern three times around the box.

- Check the surface of the box to make sure it is smooth, Sand it as needed, fill any holes with wood filler, sand it again, and use a tack cloth before painting the basecoat.

- Prepare your paint. I used the following JoSonja's Artists' Colours paints for this project:

  Chestnut
  Skin Tone Base
  Napthol Red Light
  Carbon Black
  White
  Yellow Oxide
  Pine Green
  Dark Brown or Dark Blue
  Burnt Umber

- Paint the background color in Chestnut. A lighter color of Primrose or Vellum can be substituted, if desired. See page 37 for complete instructions on adding the background color. Let the paint dry thoroughly.

- Follow the directions on page 54 for transferring the design on to the box.

I freehand-painted the tulips and leaves on the side on this box, but have included a line drawing for your use.

- Start by painting the black stripes around the bottom and middle of the box using the striper brush.

- Above the center stripe on the sides, draw the tulips with a white or gray chalk pencil. You can make some tulips elongated and others short.

- Below the center stripe, draw tulips of various sizes, leaves, and stems with the chalk pencil.

- Paint the tulips in White, Yellow Oxide, and Napthol Red Light using a number 3 or 4 round brush.

- Paint the leaves with Pine Green

Here are steps for painting the lid. Remember to allow adequate drying time between the steps.

- Begin by basing in the face and hands with Skin Tone Base using a number 2 or 3 brush; these may require several coats.

- Next, paint the boots, breeches, stripe on jacket, and hat in Black. You can also paint the black strip the man is standing on. Then paint the geometric lines at the bottom, the details to the left and right, and the dots, all in Black. To keep with the folk-art quality of the piece, these details can be done freehand. You will also use Black for the border around the image and the side edge of the lid; both should be done with a striper brush.

- Now, using White paint and a number 2 round brush, paint the shirt and band on the breeches; these may require several coats.

- Proceed to paint the jacket with Napthol Red Light. Note that the jacket is transparent over the breeches at this point.

- With Burnt Umber, paint in the small detail on the brim of the hat.

- Use a Burnt Umber and White mixture to paint in the hair.

- Then, with a Burnt Umber and Black mixture, make the cane.

- Use Yellow Oxide to paint the pocket trim, buttons, and buttonholes on the jacket. Don't forget the buttons on the back of the jacket.

Next proceed with the details of the design on the lid.

• Outline the face and hands in Burnt Umber with a fine liner or script brush.

• With a fine liner or script brush and Black paint, outline the jacket, sleeve and cuff lines, pocket trim, yellow buttons, and other jacket details. Remember to outline the larger yellow buttons on the back lower part of the jacket. Make the small buttons down the front of the white shirt.

• For the eye, paint in a miniature football shape with White. After the eye dries, use either Dark Brown or Dark Blue for the iris.

• Use a fine liner or script brush and thin Napthol Red Light for the mouth. The man has a frown on his face in the pattern, but I added a smile in my version.

• Using the fine liner, follow the face shape from the forehead down in order to define the chin. The eyebrow is a tiny comma stroke; you will need to turn your work to make this stroke. The mouth is also a comma stroke made from left to right.

• For the rosy cheeks, take a dry brush, preferably a small flat brush, dip it into the Napthol Red Light, and wipe most of the paint onto a dry paper towel. Check to make sure only a tiny bit of paint remains on the brush and barely touch it to the cheek, lightly "dusting" the area to create the effect.

Now, finish the details on the side of the box. These are all easily completed freehand.

• Outline and add the details on the flowers in White, Yellow Oxide, and Napthol Red Light, following the techniques for the various strokes on pages 38–42.

• Add details in Black to the leaves. A number 1 liner brush works well for this.

• Make dabs of Black along the stripes surrounding the box and to the top rim of the box below the lid.

• After drying, erase any chalk pencil or Saral paper lines.

• Wipe with the tack cloth.

• Finish with a coat of varnish.

• The box is an old primitive design, so I suggest that you enhance it by antiquing it. Follow the steps on page 47.

• After antiquing the box, proceed with the final varnish coats and, if desired, waxing.

PROJECT 3: *Angel*

Angels were common motifs on bride's boxes. Here is an exquisite example from a miniature box. The design is an adaptation of a box that was pictured in the Spring 2006 issue of *The Decorator*, the journal of The Historical Society of Early American Decoration.

Here are patterns for the lid. One is for the number 2 Shaker box and the other is for a number 4 Shaker box. Enlarge or reduce the size of the pattern to fit your selected box.

- Check the surface of the box to make sure it is smooth. Sand it as needed, fill any holes with wood filler, sand it again, and use a tack cloth to clean.
- Prepare your paint and paint mixes. I used the following JoSonja's Artists' Colours tube paints for this project:

> Rich Gold
> Yellow Oxide
> Naples Yellow
> Carbon Black
> Indian Red Oxide
> White
> Pearl White
> Iridescent Green
> Burgundy
> Skin Tone Base
> Green Oxide
> Rose Pink

- Base coat the box in black and then give it a second coat. See page 37 for full instructions on adding the background color.
- Mark off the bands on the lid edge and side and the bottom of the side. Paint these bands either Indian Red Oxide or Burgundy.
- Transfer the design to the box; for basic instructions, see page 54. Mark the outline of the angel, but do not include details of her gown. Make a small circle where the bouquet will be placed, as well as the three flowers at the bottom and the flower at the very top. Also make faint lines with the chalk pencil to show where the banner will go across the top.

Here are the steps for painting the lid. Be sure to allow adequate drying time between the steps.

- Start with the banners. Add a small amount of Kleister to your paint for transparency. Paint the banner directly above the angel's head in Naples Yellow mixed with Pearl White, the next in Iridescent Green, and the third in Pearl White.
- Paint the top banner in Burgundy.
- Add the circle flower in Burgundy using a number 2 or 3 flat brush.
- When the banners are dry, complete the details with a fine liner or script brush and thin White paint. First, brush-mix the Flow Medium into the White to make the spiral on the burgundy flower, then mix Burgundy with White for a rose shade for the details.
- Add teardrop strokes on both sides of the burgundy flower in either White or Pearl White.
- Across the burgundy banner, pull a series of double left comma strokes with a fine liner or script brush.
- For the other banners make continuous loops in White.
- Next paint the face, upper chest area, hands, and arms with Skin Tone Base. This may require several coats using a number 2 or 3 brush depending on the size of the box.
- With a number 3 or 4 round brush and thin Pearl White paint with a brush-mix of Kleister, begin painting the wings. Start from the outer edge and pull the strokes towards the body.
- For the bodice of the dress, make a series of left and right comma strokes with a crescent-shaped stroke at the top edge of the dress.
- Make the puffy sleeves with a series of very short strokes.
- To make the skirt, pull four left-hand comma strokes from the waist to the bottom of the gown. For the right side, make a series of right comma strokes in various lengths.
- Now, paint in the facial features. You may want to refer to pages 48–50 for full details on making faces. Start by painting the football shapes for the whites of the eyes.
- Outline the eyes with a fine line of Burnt Sienna.
- Add the color for the irises. I used Prussian Blue Hue here.
- Add a tiny white dot for the reflection spot on each eye.
- Make the eyebrows with a fine line of Burnt Sienna. An easy way to do this is to turn your work and pull the stroke for the right eyebrow from the 12 to 6 position. Likewise, turn your work again, so that the angel

is upside down, and pull the left eyebrow comma stroke from the 9 to 3 position.

- Use a fine liner or script brush with Napthol Red Light to make the lips.
- For the cheeks, use a small dry flat brush; lightly tip the brush into Napthol Red Light, remove most of the paint with a dry paper towel, and lightly dust the cheek areas.
- Make the chin line with Burnt Sienna and a 10/0 fine liner or script brush.
- For the hair, use Yellow Oxide and paint with tiny circles.
- Make tiny dots of Pearl White to create the necklace of pearls.
- Using a number 1 liner or script brush and thin White paint, paint the details on the wings and gown. These are best done freehand instead of marking details from your pattern.
- With a number 2 or 3 liner brush and Rich Gold paint, pull the pipe of the trumpet. Use right and left comma strokes to create the bell of the trumpet. You may need to adjust the fingers on the right hand once you paint the trumpet.
- For the bouquet, make small circles in transparent Yellow Oxide, with Yellow Oxide spiral overstrokes for the flowers and Green Oxide for the tiny leaves.
- Make the three flowers at the bottom with Burgundy and then add a touch of White to the burgundy to make spiral overstrokes. Use Green Oxide for the leaves.
- Add the series of loops along the bottom edge with a 10/0 script brush and thin White paint.
- On the black background surface, use an 18/0 or 10/0 script brush and thin White paint brush-mixed with Flow Medium to make the spiral, or curlicue designs.

Now you are ready to complete the flowers and details on the sides. For the miniature, because of the size of this box, only one row of tulips can be made; the original full-size box had two rows of flowers in reverse directions.

- Equally space six flowers around the side. Copy the templates on page 43; you will need to decrease the size of the templates to fit the sides.
- With the templates, use the chalk pencil to draw the outlines on the side of the box.
- Paint the flowers with Burgundy, Rose Pink, and Yellow Oxide with a number 3 brush.
- Outline the flowers in White with a fine liner or script brush.
- Paint the details of the Burgundy and pink tulips with Yellow Oxide and the yellow tulip with White.
- Pull a teardrop stroke for each stem and comma stokes for the leaves, using Green Oxide with a number 2 round brush.
- Add Yellow Oxide and White details on the leaves and stems.
- Make several randomly placed balls in Burgundy with a number 2 or 3 flat brush. Add dots in White to the center of the balls and fill in the remainder of the area with spirals in White using a fine line or script brush.
- Once your design is thoroughly dry, erase any markings, clean it with a tack cloth, and varnish. Antique if desired. Apply several more coats of varnish, wet sanding between coats, and wax if desired.

Patterns

This section of patterns is for use in creating your own bride's box design. You will find a variety of traditional patterns for a bride, a groom, different drapery designs for the top edge of your box, flowers for decoration, and fill-in designs and banners. Enlarge or decrease the patterns to adapt to your specific design. For ideas, review the Gallery of Reproduction Bride's Boxes on pages 142–172.

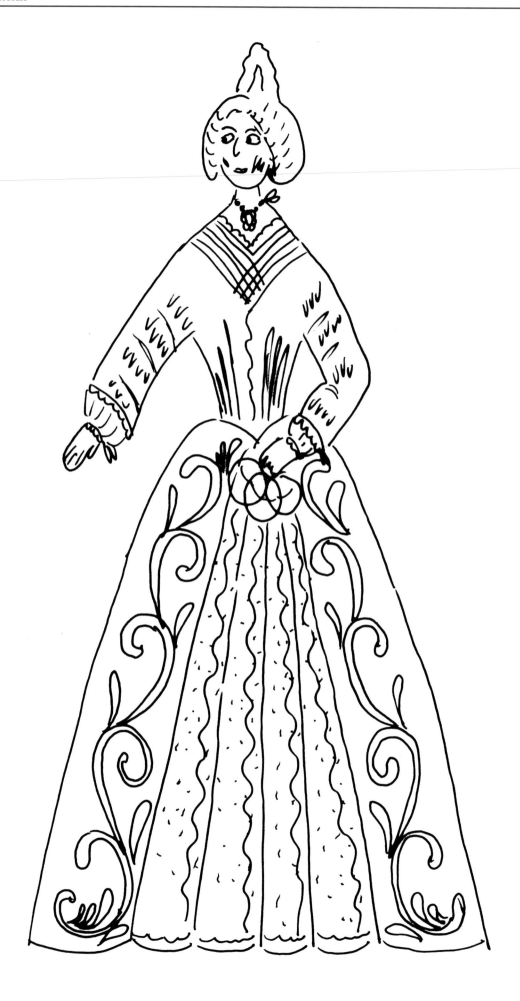

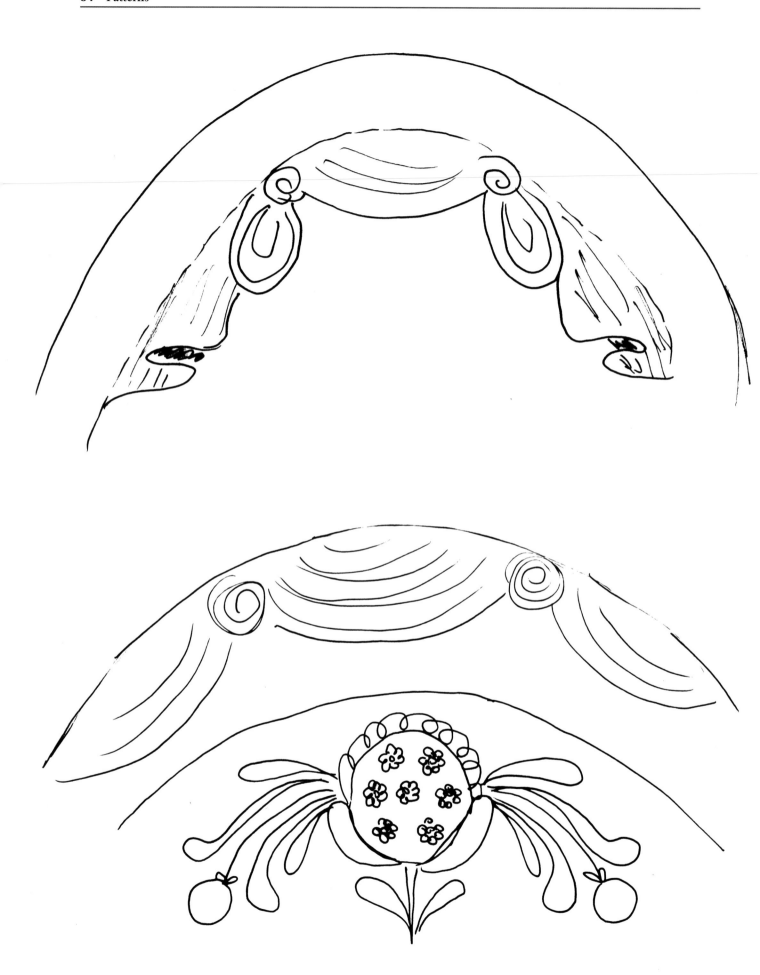

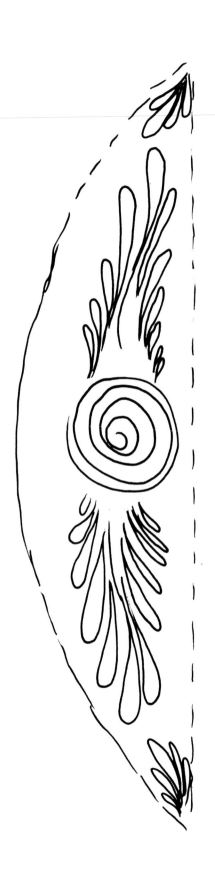

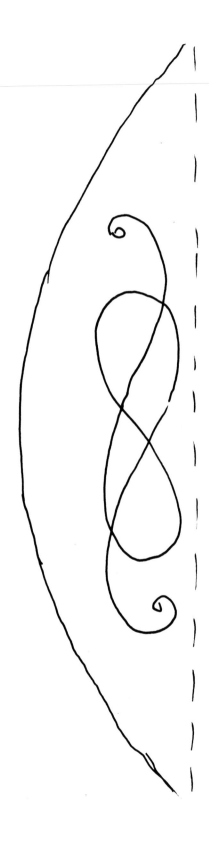

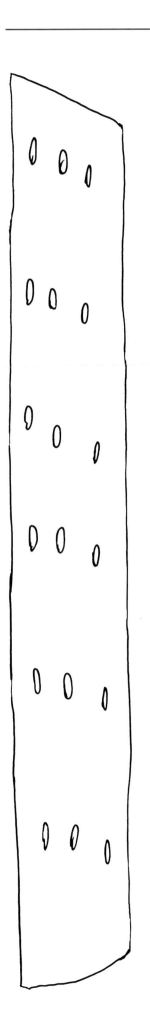
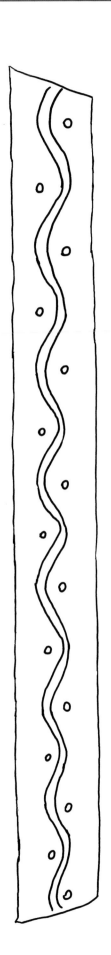

McElroy-Stoudt School Patterns

The following patterns and worksheets were given to me by Louise Diener Stoudt, a former decorative painting instructor. Both Louise and her mother, the late Lynn B. McElroy, professionally known as Esther Diener McElroy, were decorative painters who enjoyed creating bride's boxes, along with several other disciplines of Early American decorative arts. The family of the late Ruth Houser also passed on her patterns to me; she was a student of Louise Diener Stoudt. These patterns and worksheets have been prepared by these artisans.

The first two sets are flowers for bride's box sides. Both the line drawings and painted worksheets are included.

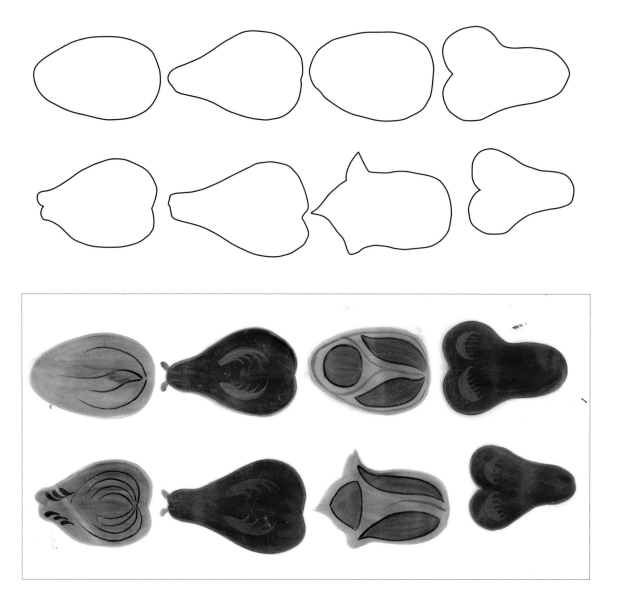

Here's a variety of patterns and painted worksheets for bride's box sides, including geometric designs and spiral fill-in strokes.

STAIN. AREA ABOVE FLOWER BAND

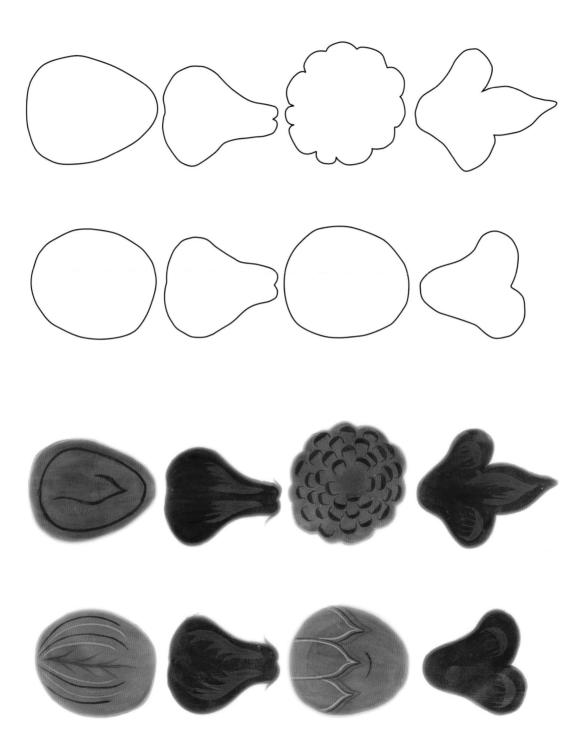

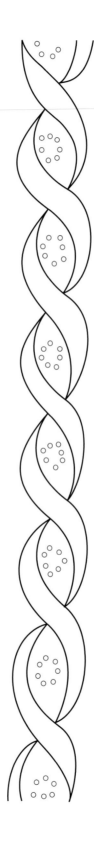

This lady in a blue coat design was painted by Louise Diener Stoudt from a box she originally saw at Landis Valley Museum. This box appears in two different versions on pages 163 and 165 in the reproduction gallery.

Bride's boxes often depicted scenes of daily life, such as this one of a man and his horse pulling a keg. Notice the keg is dated 1778. The pattern and painted worksheet of the floral design for the side is also included here.

Here are more sets of bridal couples for lids, with line
drawings and color worksheets.

This lady and goat design and its side pattern are from the collection of the William Penn Chapter of the Historical Society of Early American Decoration.

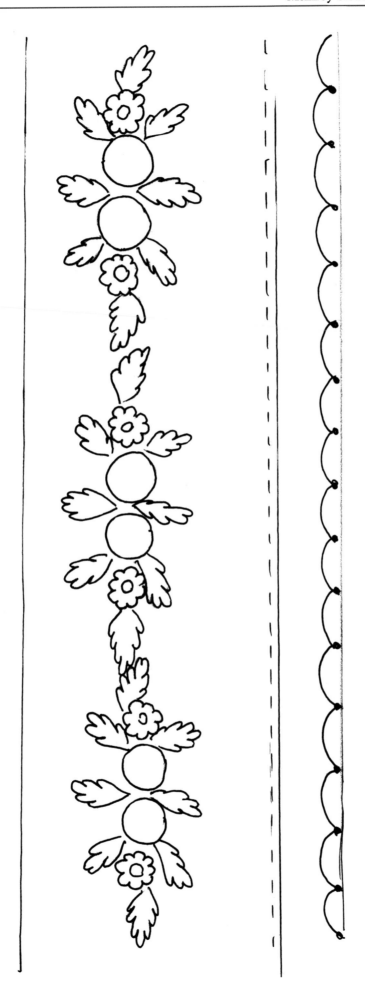

Gallery

Antique Bride's Boxes

A ntique bride's boxes are lovely treasures, and it is amazing how they have stood the test of time, some as many as two hundred years or more. Most old boxes were brought to America with the original owners when they left their homeland in regions that make up present-day Germany. Many of these were passed down within families. In southeastern Pennsylvania, where many German-speaking immigrants settled, these beautiful boxes can be found in museums, historical societies, antique shops, and auctions. In the following pages, you will find some outstanding examples.

A young, barefooted maiden holding a floral bouquet is the central figure on this oval bride's box with a light Prussian blue background. The box measures 9³/4 inches wide, 15¹/2 inches long, and 6¹/4 inches high, with a 3¹/4-inch side drop on the lid, and is laced on the right side, with both top and bottom pegged to their side pieces. The maiden is standing in a grassy area made of fine yellow comma strokes. Her dress has a long skirt, bodice, and large puffy sleeves of white with shading of pale gray, a large white collar, and a wide black belt with a gold buckle. Above the maiden are three eight-pointed stroke stars. On the lid, about ³/4 inch from the edge, is a white stripe. A dark blue border fills the space from the line to the outside edge of the lid. Blue borders are also on the top and bottom of the sides. The sides are decorated with large oval yellow ochre roses with white overstrokes, smaller vermilion circles with white overstrokes, and smaller yellow ochre circles with white overstrokes. Double white comma strokes represent the stems, and the stylized leaves are made of green oxide with white overstrokes. JOHN AND SUSAN HOYT COLLECTION

Here's another early steam-bent wooden box. This one measures $10^1/2$ inches wide, $16^3/4$ inches long, and 6 inches high, with a $3^1/2$-inch lid drop. The box is laced together on the left side and the top and bottom are pegged. The side is olive green while the top background is a beautiful ultramarine. The top has a pale pinkish $3/4$-inch border with an overstroke of burgundy on the outside edge and a white stripe on the inside edge. The center design is a lithograph of a young girl in a fancy white dress and hat playing with a hoop and a small black dog in front of a park bench. This is outlined in yellow and black stripes. The vibrant side flowers are a stylized bachelor button in pale pink, with white and red-violet overstrokes to represent the petals; a five-petal vermilion flower with yellow and burgundy stroke details; and a carnation-type flower in vermilion with yellow and burgundy overstrokes. Vermilion berries with yellow and burgundy details, green stems, and stylized leaves with yellow and white details complete the design. JOHN AND SUSAN HOYT COLLECTION

Some bride's boxes, such as this large one, were decorated in a horizontal orientation on the lid. The bridal couple here is typical of many that were rendered in a vertical design; however, all of the versions of this pair seem to have been made by the same decorator. This box has a black background. It measures 17³/4 inches long, 11³/4 inches wide, and 8 inches high. The side drop on the lid is 4 inches. The lacing is on the front of the box and the top and bottom are pegged together to their sides. The groom is seen in a three-quarter view, slightly behind the bride. He is in a military-style, thigh-length dark brown coat and knickers, with long white stockings and over-the-ankle black shoes with gold buckles. The coat has a lighter brown trim with brass buttons. The design at the very top of the box has been worn away with age, so it's difficult to tell the hairstyle or if he wore a hat. The bride is in a long pale yellow dress with vermilion inset in the skirt and a large V-shape inset at the neckline of the bodice. White overstrokes form the details of the dress. She is holding a black three-ring shape fan in her left hand.

Here again, the top is missing, so it is difficult to tell the facial features, hair styling, and type of headdress. There are large vermilion and white circles with overstrokes of white on either side of the couple along with large green comma stokes to form the flower leaves. The entire background has white curlicues of various sizes to fill in any space. Across the bottom of the lid design is a 3-inch strip of Indian red that has German printing that translates to "Remain my dear alone, you are and will always remain mine." The sides have the typical geometric-style design of vermilion, pale yellow, and white with white overstrokes for details, edged with a ¹/2-inch-wide Indian red stripe and a fine yellow stripe on either side. The side flowers are several varieties of stylized folk art flowers in vermilion and white, with white, yellow, and burgundy overstrokes along with green stems and four green leaves with yellow overstrokes for each flower. Randomly placed vermilion berries with white centers and various sizes of white curlicues or spirals complete the side details. JOHN AND SUSAN HOYT COLLECTION

This oval bride's box, also decorated in a horizontal orientation on the lid, measures 18 inches long, 11½ inches wide, and 6 inches high. The sides have a 3-inch drop to the lid. The lacing is on the front and the top and bottom are both pegged together to their sides. The design is on a vermilion background with Indian red oxide, yellow, light or sapphire blue, and white stripes around the edges of the top and sides. A 7½-by-10¼-inch lithograph of deer being chased by hunters is on the top center. This is outlined by stripes of yellow and light blue. The beautiful floral details on the sides consist of a set of two stylized flowers with four petals of white and burgundy, a six-petal burgundy flower with white and yellow details, a round yellow ochre flower with white and burgundy strokes to form the petals, and sets of burgundy flower buds with blue and white details, along with various types of stylized leaves with dark green and yellow details. JOHN AND SUSAN HOYT COLLECTION

This small trinket box measures 7⅞ inches long and 3⅝ inches high. On the lid is a simple urn dated 1804; three white flowers, each made from one teardrop and four comma strokes; and dark green stems and comma-stroke leaves with white details. The markings on either side of the urn are probably someone's initials. The sides of the lid are simply decorated with comma strokes and scrollwork details. There is no decoration on the bottom sides of the box. The background, worn away with age, may have been either painted or stained. LANDIS VALLEY MUSEUM COLLECTION

Here's another large wooden box that measures 16⁷/₈ inches long and 5³/₄ inches wide. The background appears to have been a deep burgundy red. A large blue bird with a red wing and white dot detail sits among blue folk-art tulips with white details. Other white stroke-work details complement the design. Several other flowers are barely visible, having worn away with age. A band around the top edge has also faded, but the white dots remain. The lid has a deep overlap, decorated with stylized folk-art flowers. Every other flower is a blue tulip with white details. The faded flower between was probably red with white details. Stems and leaves are in dark green with white overstrokes. Dots of black and white fill in the empty spaces. The bottom of the box is painted identically to the overlap of the lid; however, the flowers are reversed. The box is laced together with leather. LANDIS VALLEY MUSEUM COLLECTION

This small oval box with a blue background is unique. It features a diamond with an off-white insert on the center of the lid, with a light blue stripe around the edge. A fine lace-like detail in pale blue surrounds this stripe. A folk-art flower composed of dots and blue and green leaves with white details complete the center design. Each flower around the outer edge is made up of a series of dots. The sides carry through the same dot-style flowers. Both the top and bottom border designs are worn from many years of use. MERRITT'S ANTIQUES, INC.

Here's another small oval box that is very simply decorated. The design is a scene with a lady in a deep-red dress with white details. She sports a black hat and carries a walking stick, while standing on a tuft of grass with two evergreen trees in the background. Simple stroke work indicates blades of grass. The top of the box is encircled in a blue-black border with a German phrase. The sides are void of any decoration except for the narrow blue-black bands with fine yellow stripes. MERRITT'S ANTIQUES, INC.

Some boxes were designed with religious motifs, such as this one that includes a cross. Details have worn away from the faded vermilion background of this oval box, but you can still see where they were originally placed. The floral design is done in blue and white flowers along with blue stems and leaves. More details of the side flowers and borders remain. Notice the fine cross-hatching on the large flowers on the side. MERRITT'S ANTIQUES, INC.

This medium-sized oval box measures 11⅝ inches long, 6⅞ inches wide, and 5½ inches high. It is a typical European bandbox. Most of the background color is faded; however, the details of the blue and white flowers are still visible. Notice the border on the top of this box is very similar to the previous one. MERRITT'S ANTIQUES, INC.

Here's another medium-sized oval box with a dark olive-green background. The design is a floral arrangement of simple stroke-work flowers, including a tulip, folk-art roses, forget-me-nots, ball flowers, and a six-petal daisy. Leaves are green with fine yellow details for veins and decoration. A simple vermilion stripe encircles the top of the lid. The sides of the lid and bottom half of the box are also decorated in stylized folk-art flowers. The lid is laced together. MERITT'S ANTIQUES, INC.

A bright blue background lends itself well to the hunting scene on the lid of this box. A few trees and tufts of grass indicate the countryside, while small puffy white clouds make up the sky. Traces of a vermilion border outlined with a white fine scallop edge are barely visible. The box has been laced together on the side, which features sets of various stylized folk-art flowers. RON AND EILEEN RHOADES COLLECTION

This bride's box from the early 1800s is on a black background, and measures 19 inches long, 11½ inches wide, and 8 inches high. On the left side it is laced together rather than nailed. Drapery was painted around the top edge of the lid and the couple was placed atop a large heart. The groom's attire is a long red coat and pants with white trim while the bride is in a blue dress with white trim. Her headdress is vermilion and white. Between the couple are off-white flowers and on either side are large blue flowers with white trim. There are smaller flowers of different varieties on each side, with spirals to fill in the background. ROBERT J. MERRITT JR. COLLECTION

This box is very similar to the previous bride's box, with slightly different details. However, the German phrase is definitely different. This is a great comparison of how an artist can begin with the same background and create a different look by changing the details. No two things are painted identically, in the 1800s as well as today. BRIAN AND SUE HART COLLECTION

Look forward to the reproductions on pages 147–150 and compare the boxes; the details and colors are all very similar, including the side decorations. This is an original from Germany dating to the early 1800s. The box has a black background and measures 19¹/4 inches long, 12 inches wide, and 7³/4 inches high. The box is laced on the left side. ROBERT J. MERRITT JR. COLLECTION

Take a look back at the box that has the bridal couple on top of a large heart and compare the details (page 129; also compare with the box on page 130). There are many similarities, but the surrounding details are different. The boxes were most likely painted by the same artist. The colors in the clothing are reversed on this box: Now the groom is in blue and the bride in red. Above the couple is a large blue flower with white petals and smaller vermilion flowers. There is a white band around three quarters of the box, with two banner lines across the bottom. Spiral designs fill in the background of this box that measures 18 3/4 inches long, 11 5/8 inches wide, and 6 3/4 inches high. THE HISTORICAL SOCIETY OF BERKS COUNTY MUSEUM & LIBRARY, READING, PA

This box, too, may have been painted by the same artist as the previous one. Compare the details of the bridal couple. Although the man is standing partially behind the lady, the details in the clothing and facial features are almost identical. In this pose, the man has his hand on the lady's shoulder. He has a suit of Indian red oxide. She is in a gown of off-white, but the insert in her gown, the headdress, and her hairstyle are identical. The fill-in design between the man's legs is the same and the large flower details at the top are very similar. This box also includes writing on the border around the top portion of the box and two large banner areas for a German phrase across the bottom. The side flowers are also similar. RAY AND PAT OXENFORD COLLECTION

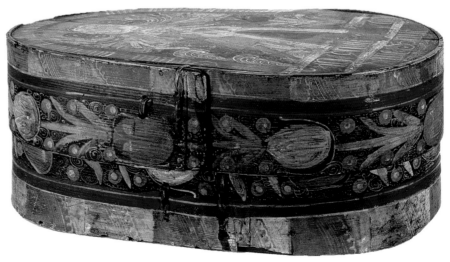

This is one of the most unusual designs to appear on the top of a bride's box. The couple stands on either side of a pillar or monument of vermilion that has white and black details. The man's body is turned to the side but his face is directed forward; he wears a long green coat, black pants, and black top hat. The lady wears a long white gown with green neckline details on the bodice and insert down the front of her gown; she also wears a top hat. The banner lines have a light blue background and are bordered with a variety of white and vermilion flowers and leaves. Spirals and white circles fill in the background. The side has the typical geometric details and flowers. THE HISTORICAL SOCIETY OF BERKS COUNTY MUSEUM & LIBRARY, READING, PA

Four large flowers, two vermilion and two off-white, and leaves complete the main design of this bride's box. The background is black and the border is Indian red oxide with yellow and white stripes. Beautiful details complement the flowers. The box has a provenance dating back to the early 1800s and is believed to have been made in Pennsylvania after the Clemmer family arrived from Germany; it remained with the family in Clayton, Berks County, for many generations. The flowers on the sides coordinate beautifully with the flowers on the top. The box has tiny white circles or balls for the background fill-in. DENNIS K. MOYER COLLECTION, THE PENNSYLVANIA FARMER, ZIONSVILLE

Amsterdam is the place of origin for this vermilion box with blue bands and white and yellow stripes. The box measures 15¹⁄₈ inches long, 9¹⁄₈ inches wide, and 5 inches high and has a lithograph of a village scene on the lid. The side includes white roses with stroke details, green stems and leaves, and small blue ball flowers. TEX JOHNSON ANTIQUES, ADAMSTOWN, PA

A cream-colored background fills this 18 1/2-inch long, 11 1/2-inch wide, and 6 1/4-inch high oval box. The man and woman are both in long robes of dark olive, with facial details in black. Notice in the close-up view that the man holds a cane in his hand. There is a blue oval in the center of the box with a German phrase, surrounded by large blue and vermilion flowers with black leaves. Small light and dark blue circles fill in the background. The side decorations are blue and vermilion flowers. TEX JOHNSON ANTIQUES, ADAMSTOWN, PA

Angels were popular designs for a bride's box. This box measures 17¼ inches long, 11½ inches wide, and 6¼ inches high. The background is black with Indian red oxide bands around the top and sides.. A continuous loop stroke completes the borders. The angel has a white gown, vermilion wings with yellow details, and long golden curly hair. The laced side has two reverse rows of flowers in vermilion and white, with yellow details. White and vermilion balls fill in the background. THURSTON NICHOLS ANTIQUES, BREINIGSVILLE, PA

This angel design is on a box measuring 17½ inches long, 10¾ inches wide, and 5½ inches high. The black background has a Indian red oxide border on the lid and sides with the continuous loop details and a yellow stripe. The angel wears a white gown with a vermilion bodice that has yellow details. The wings are transparent white with white details. Plumes at both sides of the angel and large spirals fill in the background. The side has the usual flowers, along with a combination of spirals and small white and vermilion circles. THURSTON NICHOLS ANTIQUES, BREINIGSVILLE, PA

The designs on this miniature oval box are exquisite and finely detailed. The couple appears to be dancing. The man is in a dark blue jacket and breeches with white stockings, a ruffled collar, shirt, and cuffs. The lady has a blue gown with a white bow and cuffs. The side of the box features very detailed flowers. Above the couple is the phrase "Loving Jesting and Kissing Will of no time Vex Me." The box measures 5³/₈ inches long, 4¹/₈ inches wide, and 1⁷/₈ inches high. It was most likely made in Pennsylvania, indicated by the phrase in English. Also notice that this box has a single finger lap band for the top and bottom. THURSTON NICHOLS ANTIQUES, BREINIGSVILLE, PA

This early steam-bent wooden box measures 10$^{1/4}$ inches wide, 16$^{5/8}$ inches long, and 6$^{1/4}$ inches high. It has a 3$^{1/2}$-inch drop on the lid sides. The box is laced together on the left to join the sides and pegged to join the top and bottom. The background is Indian red oxide, but shows a lot of wear on the sides, especially where one would hold it to open the box. The side design consists of an alternating solid pale yellow flower with what appears to have been a red overstroke design and a simple outline of a flower in pale yellow. Each flower has a fine yellow stem and two green leaves. The lid has a 1$^{1/4}$-inch gray border around the outside edge, with a thin black stripe on the inside. This border has a black elongated S-stroke design on top. The center section has a simple 6$^{3/4}$-inch by 5$^{1/2}$-inch rectangle of black with an outside stripe of gray. Inside the space are additional elongated S strokes. This space was probably reserved for a lithograph.

JOHN AND SUSAN HOYT COLLECTION

Reproduction Bride's Boxes

Here are several reproductions I've painted to inspire you to design your own special boxes. I have also included boxes by Ursula Erb, who is an outstanding decorative painter. All the designs are based on antique boxes and patterns, but some have slight differences. Some have been personalized as gifts. I hope the selection will give you a variety of ideas for making boxes. I prefer to just use a basic outline and then freehand all the details. Do not be intimidated by the complexity of the designs; take it step-by-step and you will succeed.

This reproduction hand-sewn bandbox is made of a fiber composition, possibly a lightweight cardboard made in the 1950 to 1960s. The design is a copy of a 1792 German bride's box. The interior has early German textbook pages as a covering, possibly pages from an old Bible. The outside is painted in a light green background. The top has a couple in the center with two white thin stripes and a white curlicue border measuring 1¼-inches around the top edges. On the left side there are teal blue and Indian Red Oxide "draperies" while the right has off-white and teal draperies. These all have overstrokes of white for decoration. The male figure has long brown straight hair and is dressed in a suit of pale gold with white over-the-ankle shoes and positioned behind the female figure; only a three-quarter view of the male is depicted. She has a teal blue skirt with Indian red oxide bodice and flounce with white overstrokes on each. Her dress has a lace collar and she wears a lace cap over her light brown hair. Her hands are invisible behind the flounce of her dress. The sides have a top and bottom border of the typical geometric design in teal blue, Indian red oxide, pale yellow, and white, with white overstrokes along a half-inch wide Indian red oxide stripe. The side center section has the light green background with three different-style folk art flowers in teal, white, yellow, and burgundy with white or red overstrokes. Green leaves and stems complete this design. A few white curlicues complement the light green background sections. JOHN AND SUSAN HOYT COLLECTION

This is one of my first boxes. It was a project in a class I took from Jackie Shaw of Hagerstown, Maryland, in the fall of 1988, just weeks before our daughter's wedding. We were given an unpainted box and asked to create a floral design of our choice. The box measures 9 1/2 inches long, 12 inches wide, and 5 1/2 inches high. It is a nontraditional box with woven sides. The base color is a rose pink, with light pink top border. I created a stroke floral design, and as I was painting this in that class I decided to include the inscription around the top edge. I gave this to our daughter and son-in-law to commemorate their wedding. It is the perfect storage place for Kelly's bridal bouquet. KELLY AND MATTHEW SIMMONS COLLECTION

For my cousin's fiftieth wedding anniversary, I created a bride's box from a large Shaker box I purchased. The background is a marbleized burgundy, with golden yellow drapery across the top, and urns of golden yellow tulips on either side of the bridal couple. Although the figures are in eighteenth-century attire, I added some details that identify the couple. The groom is in a military-style blue suit to honor his service in World War II and he holds a Bible because he was a retired minister. The bride is attired in a golden yellow skirt with burgundy bodice with lace trim, apron, and hat. The lower banner line honors their anniversary with an angel and the years of their wedding and fiftieth celebration. Around the top edge of the lid is the full wedding date, their names, and the blessing, "Love is the Greatest Joy on Earth." There are geometric borders on both the top and bottom edges of the side, with a row of multi-color tulips, stems, leaves, and spiral fill-in strokes.

REV. DENTON AND LA RUE SPENCER COLLECTION

This box is 18 inches long, 13½ inches wide, and 9 inches high. I adapted the design from a JoSonja pattern. It has a dark blue background, burgundy border with yellow oxide comma strokes and dots, and a white stripe. Transparent white drapery is across the top, and tulips bloom beside the bridal couple. The bride's gown is pine green with yellow oxide details, burgundy bodice with white details, and transparent white apron, collar, and cap with white details. The groom has black boots, brown pants, and a raw sienna coat with green, burgundy, and white trim. His hair is yellow oxide. The angel also has yellow oxide hair, with wings of transparent white. The burgundy heart states "Liebe," which translates to "love." The side has a geometric border around the top edge and a double row of tulips in various styles and colors with white details. White spirals fill in the background. BRENT AND SARAH WHITE COLLECTION

This design was often repeated on early bride's boxes. You will find an original on page 131.

This adaptation is on a box that measures 19 inches long, 11^3/$_4$ inches wide, and 6^1/$_2$ inches high. The black background has an opaque white drape across the top with a double row of Indian red oxide banners across the bottom with a German inscription. The bride is dressed in pale yellow with vermilion inset in the skirt and trim on the bodice, with pale yellow and vermilion details. She wears a white lace cap and holds a black fan. The groom sports an Indian red oxide jacket with gold oxide breeches, white stockings, and black shoes. Vermilion buttons and yellow trim enhance his jacket and he wears a black hat. A large stylized vermilion flower with yellow details is beside the man, but there is only space for a small flower beside the lady. Pale gold oxide stems and leaves with large circular white flowers with red and gold oxide trim are at either side of the bridal couple. Notice that the circular design at the bottom is actually off center. Large white spirals or squiggles fill in the background. The side has geometric designs on the top and bottom, with a single row of stylized flowers in Napthol red light and white with yellow oxide, burgundy, and white details. Pale yellow stems have gold oxide details. Both top and side have the small circles of burgundy with white dots. The inscription in German translates to "May my love live forever, peace in the home is best and makes it possible to eat, where as quarreling causes everything to go awry." BRIAN AND DORIS HETTINGER COLLECTION

This adaptation on a small box was created for a fiftieth anniversary. The box measures 13^1/$_2$ inches long, 8^3/$_8$ inches wide, and 6^1/$_4$ inches high. The background is black with Deep Plum from JoSonja's Background Colours for the two banners on the lid and stripe color around the top and bottom of the side. The top has a semitransparent white drape, with a large round white flower with yellow oxide and burgundy trim, green oxide stems, and leaves with yellow oxide details. There are several round burgundy balls, each with a white dot on either side of the bridal couple. The lady's gown is Naples yellow hue with a yellow oxide insert and bodice trim. There is transparent white lace around the V–shaped neckline and sleeve cuffs. The bottom inset on the dress has an overskirt of transparent lace. She also wears a lace cap. Both the dress and cap have rich gold details; she also holds a gold fan. The man sports a suit of burnt sienna with yellow oxide details and rich gold buttons; his breeches are yellow oxide. He has white stockings, neckline, and sleeve ruffles and black shoes and hat, each with rich gold details. The couple's names are in the top banner and their wedding date in the bottom banner. A wavy green stroke with details of yellow oxide and white, along with burgundy balls, separate the

two banners, while the bottom has white detailed strokes to encompass "50th Anniversary" in rich gold. The side geometric details are in gold oxide, yellow oxide, and Naples yellow hue with white details. Flowers are in white and yellow oxide with green oxide stems, leaves trimmed with Naples yellow hue, and white and yellow oxide details. Burgundy balls with white dots and white spirals fill in the background details. The inside has a faux finish of yellow oxide and white, with a large heart in the inside top of the lid that includes a personal blessing in German. This box has been antiqued.

FAMILY OF ELIZABETH ANDERSON COLLECTION

Here's another box with this same design as the previous one; however this is smaller in size and therefore has a slight variation of details. The large white flowers on either side of the couple are slightly different, as are the details on the gown. The printing is in the Old German style. The side view shows the finger lap attachment. The inside has a faux finish with a personal inscription to the couple. WILLIAM AND AMY MASON COLLECTION

This large box, 19¼ inches long, 12 inches wide, and 7¾ inches deep, has a design that was adapted from an article by Linda Carter Lefko in the June 2004 issue of *Early American Life*. It has a moss-green background, yellow oxide details, a red heart with white details between the couple, and a large round floral motif with yellow oxide trim above the heart. The names and date are printed in white. The bride has a ruby-red dress with yellow oxide details, dark green insert in the skirt and bodice, and white lace around the neckline. She has a green headdress with red and green details. The groom is attired in a yellow-green suit with dark green details with yellow trim. His hair is in spiral curls. The sides have various flowers in yellow, burgundy, and blue with green leaves with yellow details. There is a yellow oxide band around both the top and bottom of the sides. The inside has a faux finish with a message of "Love . . . Today I will marry my friend." DON AND DEBRA UHRIG

This one has a blue background. The top features sheer white curtains and detailed flowers beside the couple. Here the bride has a light blue gown with a fan-like lace insert in the skirt and a ruffle lace insert in the bodice with lace neckline and lace cap. The full sleeve has lace-edge trim and dark blue and white details. She also wears a pearl white necklace and holds a gold fan. The groom, who is much taller than her, has a brown suit and breeches with white stockings and black shoes. At the bottom, an angel holds a heart that states "Liebe" ("love"). The printing of the names and dates matches the style from the couple's wedding invitation. A series of detailed comma strokes enhance the bottom. Burgundy balls with yellow oxide centers and white spiral strokes fill in the background on the lid. The lid also has a border of comma strokes around the top edge. The side has variations of ball flowers with white and burgundy details and green leaves with gold oxide trim. A faux finish complements the inside with a special message from the groom's parents. The gift box held a handkerchief from the groom's grandmother who was from Germany. JARED AND BRE MYERS COLLECTION

Light background boxes are not seen as frequently as the dark or black background boxes. This particular design is an adaptation from several different boxes. The bride's parents liked various things from three different boxes, so those aspects were combined to create this design. The background color is Linen from JoSonja's Background Colours, with burgundy banners across the bottom and a fine stripe around the top edge. The center heart and large flower designs were taken from the green background box on page 151. The flowers beside the couple are from another box, and the pose of the bridal couple from yet a different design. The bridal gown is warm white with yellow oxide neckline details and a transparent white lace edge. The skirt inset is vermilion with transparent lace overskirt details and yellow oxide details on the skirt and bodice. The gown has full sleeves with lace details. The bride holds a fan in her hand. The groom has a light brown long jacket with gold buttons and dark brown details and breeches. White stockings extend above his high black boots with gold buckles. His shirt has a ruffled neck band and sleeves. Warm white details of a spiral flower and stroke work details complete the bottom of the lid design. Just a few spirals surround the outer edge of the lid. The side details on the top and bottom are geometric borders and a central band is decorated with a variety of flowers in white and vermilion with burgundy, yellow oxide, and white trim. Stems and leaves are green oxide with yellow oxide details. JAMES AND KAREN PAUCIELLO COLLECTION

Here's a black background box created from several different designs selected by the bride's mother to create this special large-sized bride's box. The floral designs on either side of the bridal couple have appeared in several other boxes, but this time the flowers are in Naples yellow hue with red details. The bride has a very full, light blue gown with white lace inset in the bodice, the trim around the neckline, and the cuffs of her sleeves. Rows of lace overlay a light blue background. Blue ribbon details complement the neckline, waist, and sleeves. The bride wears a lace cap and her shoulder-length brown hair is visible. Her jewelry is a gold broach and pearl necklace. The groom has a dark brown jacket with lighter brown breeches and details on the jacket. He has a white ruffled collar and cuffs on his shirt and a dark brown hat. The black shoes have gold buckles, and he wears white knee-length stockings. A heart with "Liebe" is at the bottom with white stroke-work details. Fine white spirals surround the outer edge of the top and bottom portion of the lid. A geometric design of burgundy, light blue, pale yellow, and light green with white details surrounds the bottom and top edge of the side. Warm white and pale yellow flowers with red, white, and yellow oxide details are around the side with green leaves and stems with lighter green details. Burgundy balls with white centers and white spirals fill in the background of the sides. NICHOLAS AND STACY DEDRING COLLECTION

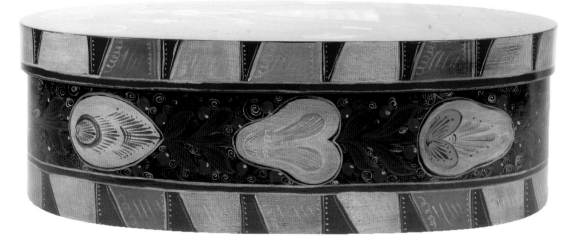

This is another box designed from parts of several other antique boxes. The light background design is decorated with burgundy drapery at the top and two banners at the bottom. The heart between the couple is burgundy with stylized tulips and dogwood-style flowers in shades ranging from pink to burgundy. The gown is a rose pink with an inset of vermilion and a sheer lace overlay on the entire dress. All the details of the gown—the lace cap, necklace, and broach—are in white. She holds a burgundy fan in her left hand. The groom's long jacket is chestnut with dark brown trim and gold buttons. He has a white ruffled collar and cuffs. The breeches are dark brown, and he wears white stockings and black shoes with gold buckles. The side has a geometric top and bottom border in pink, burgundy, green oxide, and vermilion, with warm white details. Flowers are in the same colors with warm white details and green oxide leaves. Small vermilion balls and warm white spirals fill in around the edges of the lid and side. The box has been antiqued and the inside has a faux finish, including a large heart with personal wishes included.

JOHN AND BRYNN TATAROWICZ COLLECTION

Some bride's boxes added the couple to a scene, such as this one that I painted on a large Shaker box. I adapted this design from an original box acquired by the Society of Decorative Painters for their Decorative Arts Collection in 2000 and featured in the March/April 2001 issue of *The Decorative Painter*. This adaptation design is on a much smaller box than the original, a circa 1820 box that was purchased from an antique shop in Germany. The band on the lid is in a dark blue with yellow and white stripes around. The side is in burgundy and has flower buds in rose, with burgundy and warm white details and green leaves with yellow trim. It also has a faux finish interior. RAY AND PAT OXENFORD COLLECTION

The design of the lady and her goat is taken from an old German bride's box. Several years ago the William Penn Chapter of the Historical Society of Early American Decoration painted bride's box replicas for table favors, and this was one of the designs. On this small oval Shaker–style box, I painted a blue-gray sky and shades of brown for the earth. There are a few green and white comma strokes with yellow dots for foliage. The lady wears a dark blue skirt with white blouse and dark blue and Indian red oxide trim. Her large-brimmed hat is white with Indian red oxide details. She carries a long staff as she tends her goat. The side is Indian red oxide embellished with small flowers in blue, vermilion, and burgundy, with blue-stroke leaves with yellow details. A white stripe and comma stroke pattern complete the side details. The German translation is "My goat, the special dear, gives only milk but no beer." A pattern for this design is included on page 112.

RAY AND PAT OXENFORD COLLECTION

Here's the lady and her goat design, personalized and adapted for a small keepsake box to commemorate the birth of a child. I've painted the traditional lady, adjusted the background, and used a photograph of the family pet to replace the goat. The border around the lid edge and banners are in yellow oxide with white details. An angel, conveying love, along with the name and birth date, complete the lid. The side has the geometric top and bottom border in blue, yellow-green, and warm white. The central part has a burgundy background and a variety of flowers and leaves with the white spiral details for fill-in. The interior has a faux finish with a heart incorporated in the interior lid design to include the birth information. THE KINNEY FAMILY COLLECTION

This is another variation of the previous box. The lady's clothing colors vary slightly with different details. The family pet also has been included, and the angel details are changed. The side details are similar, with a change in colors and styles of flowers. The interior also has a faux finish with a heart and the birth information included. THE PETERS FAMILY COLLECTION

The horse and rider theme was used for a young man's keepsake box. The shaded blue background with dark blue borders and banners complement the white horse and rider. The horseman is in a blue suit and hat with red trim. There is a spray of flowers at the top and bottom of the lid and these same flowers are also on the side of the box. The side also has a broad burgundy ribbon stripe with thin yellow stripe and white comma strokes. A complementary faux finish completes the interior of the box along with birth information honoring the young man. THE KINNEY FAMILY COLLECTION

Here's another style of the horse and rider theme on a keepsake box. A medium blue background with dark blue border and banners set the tone for the gray horse and young rider. The horse has an emblem with the young man's initials. The young man is wearing gold oxide pants and a blue jacket and hat. Ball flowers with stroke-work details complete the design. These same flowers complement the side designs. The inside has a faux finish with a heart for the child's birth information. THE PETERS FAMILY COLLECTION

Not all boxes are oval. This 6-inch round box is another design prepared several years ago by the William Penn Chapter of the Historical Society of Early American Decoration. The painting began with a cherry stain that was then overpainted for the design background, which is black and brown with some green to represent grass. A couple dancing is the main theme, with white comma strokes around the edge of the lid. The side has a geometric border around the top edge, with a variety of strokes on a black background to create the remainder of the design. The German translation is "Beautiful Gredel dear, let's both make merry here."

RAY AND PAT OXENFORD COLLECTION

Here's a box featuring a lady in her winter finery. I had received this pattern from Louise Diener Stoudt and painted it on a two-finger high box. The design is on a blue background. The artist who originally designed this most likely painted it several different ways. Recently a box with this same design painted on a stained background with no designs on the side came up at a local auction. I have painted a variety of flowers in burgundy, pink, and yellow on the side with green leaves and a burgundy shield with white details around the edge of the lid. The German translation is "Lonesome and alone should my fate never be" at the top and "Love" at the bottom. You will notice a variation of this same design in the box that was painted by Ursula Erb, as well as another version of it in the pattern section on page 98.

RAY AND PAT OXENFORD COLLECTION

This is a bride's box made by the late J. R. Stoudt and painted by his wife, Louise Diener Stoudt, in 1976. It measures 16¹/2 inches long, 10¹/2 inches wide, and 5¹/2 inches high. The design is a copy of an antique box, and the pattern is included on page 114. An antique box of this same design is on page 132. This design is painted on a black background with the groom in a green suit with white trim and the bride in an Indian red oxide gown with black inset in the skirt and white details. Green and Indian red oxide flowers complement the details with a geometric top and bottom border on the side. White spirals fill in the background. The German translation is "Love me only or let me go." PAINTED BY LOUISE DIENER STOUDT

Each artist interprets designs differently. Here, Ursula Erb has painted the lady in her winter finery in a dark blue coat with fur trim and muff with a long light blue skirt. The side is stained with bands around top and bottom and beautifully executed flowers in the middle. The German around the edge of the lid translates to "Lonesome and alone shall myself suffice." The box measures 16 inches long, 9¼ inches wide, and 6½ inches high. See page 98 for this pattern. PAINTED BY URSULA ERB

This 11³/₄-inch round bride's box is 5¹/₂ inches high and taken from an old German design of lovers sitting on a rock with stylized tulips on either side. A dark green background complements the design with a geometric border along the upper edge of the side and a variety of flowers around the bottom of the box. The German translation is "All my love shall be directed to you only." PAINTED BY URSULA ERB

Man and his best friends, the dog and horse, are depicted on this box that has a stained background over-painted with blue. A variety of white and vermilion flowers, along with green leaves, adorns the bottom and side of the box. Black bands with white details complement the side. The German translation is "I am traveling to America, were it better, I'd stay." PAINTED BY URSULA ERB

Flowers appear over the entire surface of this box. The lid has an urn from which the flowers radiate, while the side is decorated with two rows of flowers. A white stripe runs along the inside edge of the outer band of the lid, while three bands surround the side. Each band has a series of strokes in white and yellow oxide. The box measures 18 inches long, 13$\frac{1}{2}$ inches wide, and 8$\frac{3}{4}$ inches high. PAINTED BY URSULA ERB

A traditional bridal couple appear on this black background box that is 18¼ inches long, 13½ inches wide, and 9 inches high. Plumes emerge on both sides of the bridal couple. Spirals fill in the background details. A double white stripe and a continuous loop design surround the lid. The side has a geometric design around the top and the bottom edge with stylized tulips in complementary colors and fine details, including the green stems and leaves, running in the center. Berries and white spirals fill in the background details. The German translation is "When two love one another everything will turn out for the best." PAINTED BY URSULA ERB

This old design was created directly from the original on page 114, but here the heart is the central design with the bridal couple above it. Green drapery is across the top of the black-background box, which is 18 inches long, 13¹/₂ inches wide, and 9 inches high. Large flowers are on either side of the heart, with the spiral details filling in the background. The side has the common geometric designs on top and bottom, with a variety of flowers along with stems, leaves, and berries running through the center. The spirals complete the background details. The translation of the German inscription within the heart is "My heart alone or leave me be!" PAINTED BY URSULA ERB

Here's an unusual design of a man between two ladies. Which shall he choose? Both ladies are dressed in elegant dresses. Plumes are on each side of the lid, with spirals filling in the background. The side has an upper geometric border along with stylized flowers in complementary colors. Spiral strokes fill in the background. The translation of the German is "My heart alone or leave me be!" The box measures 18 inches long, 13½ inches wide, and 8¾ inches high. PAINTED BY URSULA ERB

The man on horseback was a common design, but rare on boxes. Beautifully detailed scenery surrounds the sides of this elegant box that measures 15 inches long, 9 inches wide, and 7¹/₂ inches high. The German inscription around the top edge of the lid translates to "Do spare your young life, why do you want to give it for others." PAINTED BY URSULA ERB

Supplies and Resources

Supplies

Ace Hardware Corporation
866-920-5334
www.acehardware.com
Miscellaneous supplies, painter's tape, sanding supplies

A.C. Moore
www.acmoore.com
Paints, brushes, art supplies

Artist's Club
800-845-6507
www.ArtistsClub.com
Paints, brushes, miscellaneous supplies, books, pattern packets

Chroma Inc. USA
205 Bucky Drive
Lititz, PA 17543
717-626-8866
www.chromaonline.com
Manufacturer of the JoSonja's paints and mediums

Dick Blick Art Materials
P.O. Box 1267
Galesburg, IL 61402-1267
800-447-8192
www.dickblick.com
Paints, mediums, art supplies, brushes

JoSonja's
2136 Third Street
Eureka, CA 95501
www.josonja.com
Books, pattern packets, brushes, seminars

Linda Carter Lefko
www.lclefko.com
Pattern packets

Michael's
www.michaels.com
Paints, brushes, art supplies

Museum Books Inc.
P.O. Box 5977
Wyomissing, PA 19610
610-372-0642
museumbooks@1usa.com
Out-of-print books

Old Village Paint Ltd.
P.O. Box 1030
Fort Washington, PA 19034
610-238-9001
Basecoat paint

Ray Oxenford
805 Hill Drive
Douglassville, PA 19518
610-385-3431
paoxenford@dejazzd.com
Unpainted bride's boxes, repairs

Parker Paint Inc.
1058 Arnold Road
Reading, PA 19605
610-396-9763
www.shadesof76.com
RJParker@shadesof76.com
Historic paint colors, colors matched

Scharff Brushes, Inc.
P.O. Box 746
Fayetteville, GA 30214
888-SCHARFF, 770-461-2200
SCHARFF@ARTBRUSH.com
www.ARTBRUSH.com
Brushes and quills

Steph's Folk Art Studio LLC
232 Hartman Bridge Road
P.O. Box 309
Strasburg, PA 17579
717-687-7520
www.stephsfolkart.com
JoSonja's paints, mediums, pattern packets, and classes

Utrecht Art Supplies
6 Corporate Drive
Cranbury, NJ 08512
www.utrechtart.com
All types of painting and art supplies

John Wilson
406 East Broadway Highway
Charlotte, MI 48813
517-543-5325
www.ShakerOvalBox.com
Copper tacks, steam trays, videos, classes

Organizations

**Historical Society of Early
American Decoration**
Farmers' Museum
P.O. Box 30
Cooperstown, NY 13326
866-304-7323
www.HSEAD.org

Society of Decorative Painters
393 North McLean Blvd.
Wichita, KS 67203-5968
316-269-9300

Museums and Historic Sites

Many museums and historic sites
have specialized collections of folk
art that include bride's boxes.

**Abby Aldrich Rockefeller
Folk Art Museum**
325 West Francis Street
Williamsburg, VA 23185
www.history.org/history/museums/
abby_art.cfm

American Folk Art Museum
45 West 53rd Street
New York, NY 10019
212-265-1040
www.folkartmuseum.org

**The Historical Society of Berks
County Museum & Library**
940 Centre Avenue
Reading, PA 19601
610-375-4375
www.berkshistory.org

Landis Valley Museum
2451 Kissel Hill Road
Lancaster, PA 17601
717-569-0401
www.landisvalleymuseum.org

Reading Public Museum
500 Museum Road
West Reading, PA 19611
610-371-5850
www.readingpublicmuseum.org

**Winterthur Museum,
Garden, & Library**
Route 52
Winterthur, DE 19735
800-448-3883
www.winterthur.org

Antique Dealers and Auction Houses

Many antique dealers and auction
houses of southeastern Pennsylvania
usually have a good supply of antique
bride's boxes for sale.

Alderfer Auction & Appraisal
501 Fairgrounds Road
Hatfield, PA 19440
215-393-3000
www.alderferauction.com

Meeting House Square Antiques
Stoudt's Black Angus
Adamstown, PA 19501
717-898-6381

**The Pennsylvania Farmer Antiques
and Folk Art**
4640 Church View Road
Zionsville, PA 18092-2001
610-965-5146

**Pook & Pook Inc., Auctioneers
and Appraisers**
463 East Lancaster Avenue
Downingtown, PA 19335
610-269-4040
www.pookandpook.com

Tex Johnson Antiques
40 Willow Street
Box 864
Adamstown, PA 19501
717-484-4005 or 610-372-1198
www.texjohnsonantiques.com

**Thurston Nichols American
Antiques Inc.**
610-972-4563
www.antiques101.com

Bibliography

Anderson, Lia. *Schachteln Boxes by Lia: Inspirations from the Museums of Europe.* Springfield, VA: Bavarian Folk Art by Lia, 1995.

Brazer, Esther Stevens. "Antique Decoration: Pennsylvania Bride Boxes and Dower Chests," *Antiques*, 1925.

"Bentwood for a Bride." *The Decorative Painter* 2, no. 2 (March/April 2001): 32.

Cummins, Genevieve. "Antique Boxes, Inside and Out." *The Decorator* 60, no. 1 (Spring 2006): 16–20.

Droge, Kurt, and Pretzell, Lothar. *Bemalte Spanschachteln.* Munich: Callwey, 1986.

Edwards, Sybil. *Decorative Folk Art.* Newton-Abbot, UK: David & Charles, 1994.

Folk Art Furniture and Accessories. Vol. 4. Pipka's Publications, 1988.

Halverson, Deborah. "The Coffin House." *Early American Life* 10, no. 3 (June 1979): 44–47.

Jansen, JoSonja. "Gifts from the Heart." *Artist's Journal* 44 (Spring 2001): 16–19.

Kauffman, Henry J. *Pennsylvania Dutch American Folk Art.* Rev. ed. Elverson, PA: Self-published, 1993.

Lefko, Linda Carter. "German Decorated Boxes." *Early American Life* 35, no. 3 (June 2004): 22–26.

Marston, Jeanne. "Decorate a Bride's Box." *Early American Life* 25, no. 3 (June 1994): 62–63.

Pennsylvania Dutch Folk Arts: Philadelphia Museum of Art from The Geesey Collection and Others. Philadelphia: Philadelphia Museum of Art, 1956.

Wascher, Herta. *Ornamental Painted Boxes.* Rosenheim, Germany: Thorsons Publishing Group, 1983.